Office 97

A progressive course for
new users

Steve Hill

Senior Lecturer in Information
Systems at Staffordshire University

Letts
1997

A CIP record for this book is available from the British Library.

ISBN 1 85805 223 8

Copyright © Steve Hill, 1997

Editorial and production services: Genesys Editorial Limited
Typeset by Ian Foulis & Associates, Saltash, Cornwall.

Printed in Great Britain by Martins the Printers, Berwick upon Tweed

Contents

About this book

Aims

This book provides an introduction for users of Office 97 standard and professional editions, and includes coverage of Word, Excel, Access, PowerPoint and Outlook for the most commonly performed tasks. It does not cover the Windows 95 operating environment, nor does it cover all features of the Office applications. Readers who want to find out more about either Windows 95 or advanced uses of the Office applications are advised to refer to the extensive on-line help available, and to Letts Educational's other books on individual Office applications and Windows 95.

The book is suitable for all beginners of Office 97, whether home or work users. It covers all tasks required for introductory RSA and City & Guilds courses in the major business applications. It is also suitable for those thinking of purchasing Office 97 who want a summary of its main features and its hardware and software requirements.

However, while there are many books on Office and its components, including other excellent books by Letts Educational, they cover much more material than is needed by introductory users. This book is tailored to the most common tasks performed using the Microsoft Office applications.

Structure

The book is made up of self-contained modules for Word, Excel, Access, Power-Point and Outlook.

Each module is divided into units which:

- state the learning objectives

- cover the procedures for meeting those objectives

- provide practical exercises to reinforce the learning activities

- make extensive use of screen dumps to help users check that they are following procedures correctly

- provide useful advice and tips on alternative and short-cut methods of working with the applications (indicated by a 🔘 icon).

The units within each module should be worked through in sequence, but the applications can be worked through in any order.

Section 1: Word 97 for Windows

All the information you need to carry out every-day tasks with Word 97 is presented here.

To do this	Turn to...
Start and exit from Word	Unit 1 Starting Word 97 for Windows
Open and move around a document	Unit 1 Starting Word 97 for Windows
Enter, delete and replace text	Unit 2 Starting a new document
Spell check a document	Unit 2 Starting a new document
Save a document	Unit 2 Starting a new document
Change the layout and format of a document	Unit 3 Text and document layout and formatting
Move and copy text	Unit 4 Moving and copying blocks of text
Print documents	Unit 5 Printing your work
Use templates and wizards	Unit 5 Printing your work

Section 2 Excel 97

All the information you need to carry out every-day tasks with Excel 97 is presented here.

To do this	Turn to...
Start and exit from Excel	Unit 6 Introduction to Excel 97
Find an existing spreadsheet	Unit 6 Introduction to Excel 97
Open and save a workbook	Unit 7 Opening and using a workbook
Move to a cell in a workbook	Unit 7 Opening and using a workbook
Enter, copy and move data	Unit 8 Creating a new workbook
Generate values using formulae and functions	Unit 9 Using formulae and functions
Use absolute and relative cell addressing	Unit 9 Using formulae and functions
Format a spreadsheet	Unit 10 Formatting spreadsheets
Print a spreadsheet	Unit 11 Printing and layout
Change the format for printing	Unit 11 Printing and layout
Create and edit charts and graphs	Unit 12 Creating charts and graphs in Excel

Section 3: Access 97

All the information you need to carry out every-day tasks with Access 97 is presented here.

To do this	Turn to...
Start Access	Unit 13 Introduction to databases and Access 97
Use Help	Unit 13 Introduction to databases and Access 97

Section 4: PowerPoint 97

All the information you need to carry out every-day tasks with PowerPoint 97 is presented here.

Section 5: Outlook

All the information you need to carry out every-day tasks with Outlook is presented here.

Additional information

At the end of the book you will find the following:

■ Summary of shortcuts: A quick reference guide to keys, buttons and menus which are used for common tasks.

■ Glossary: A list of definitions of common terms used.

■ Index.

Conventions

Terminology

The terms 'DOS' and 'MS-DOS' are used interchangeably.

The terms 'PC', 'personal computer' and 'computer' are used interchangeably.

Typographical conventions

Menu and dialog boxes items are shown as: File

Buttons are shown as: **Save**

Keys on the keyboard are shown as: *ctrl /A*

Names of files, fields, reports and other items created by the user are shown as **Employee**

Text that you type in yourself is in Times typeface which looks like this.
(Note that text can be typed in upper or lower case.)

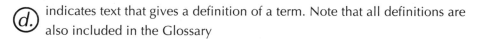 indicates text that gives a definition of a term. Note that all definitions are also included in the Glossary

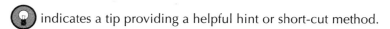 indicates a tip providing a helpful hint or short-cut method.

indicates a cautionary note.

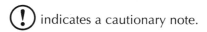 indicates a cross reference.

A note to lecturers and students

The minimal manual approach

This book adopts a minimal manual approach: only what is required to meet learning objectives is covered, so avoiding overloading users with extraneous knowledge of unnecessary (at this level) commands and procedures. This is an approach to learning originally developed at IBM's laboratories in the 1980s and extensively proven to reduce both the size of the book and learning time.

The active-learning approach

Research evidence shows that users learn best when they are actively problem solving, rather than passively watching animated demonstrations and tutorials of the software's procedures. Throughout the book users are required to make use of problem-solving procedures, and to undertake guided exploration on their own.

Users make mistakes

Most books assume error-free performance from users who follow instructions to the letter, in sequence and without making mistakes. Experience, however, shows that such users rarely exist. It's normal to make mistakes, and is an important way of learning. The approach taken here, based on observations of users performing these tasks, is to note common errors and mistakes that are made and to offer advice on how to recover from them, why they happened and how to avoid them in the future.

What else do you need?

This section contains some technical terms, and is intended to help you decide whether you can run Office 97 on your present computer. Don't worry if you don't understand the terms, just ask a knowledgeable friend (or PC salesperson) to explain them to you.

Office 97 is available in standard and professional versions, the latter including the Access database package. Although it is sometimes claimed that it is possible to run Office on a computer with a 486-SX processor and 8Mb of RAM memory, this is totally unrealistic. A usable minimum specification is a 486-DX4 computer and 8Mb for the standard edition, and 12Mb for Office Professional. However, 16Mb is strongly recommended as a workable minimum. You also need approximately 100Mb of hard disk space for the standard version, and 140Mb for the professional version. You need to make sure that your hard disk has an additional 30Mb of space for Windows 95 to use as a swap-file. You also need the Windows 95 operating system already installed on your computer. Because of the size of the software, it is easier to load the CD version, in which case you will need a CD-ROM drive.

In summary, here are the recommended hardware and software requirements:

- Windows 95 or NT

- 150Mb disk space minimum

- Pentium processor minimum

- 16Mb RAM

- CD-ROM drive

Should I upgrade from Office 95 or Office 4?

Office 97 is largely a re-write of Office 95 with better integration with the Internet, so in fact it offers relatively few additional features for introductory users. Probably the most noticeable significant feature is the World-Wide-Web integration. Of course, it does contain some new features, but these are not in the main of much relevance to introductory users of the package.

Office 4 runs perfectly well under Windows 95, and even has a look and feel very similar to Office 97 when run under Windows 95. Most users are unlikely to notice any significant differences in the speed of the two versions for the tasks covered in this book, so the author's personal advice to Office 4 users is to only upgrade if there are particular features of Office 97 (such as the ability to map geographical data in Excel, or improved database optimisation tools) that they particularly want. You should also take into account that Office 4 runs quite happily with 8Mb of RAM, compared with a realistic minimum of 16Mb for Office 97.

Installing Office 97

Before installing Office 97, read the section above on Office 97 hardware and software requirements.

1 Close any applications that are running.

2 Disable any anti-virus software if applicable.

3 Insert the CD (or floppy disk 1) into the appropriate drive. The following screen will appear:

4 Double–click Setup.exe to start the Office 97 setup. If the screen doesn't appear, click the **Start** button, then click **Run** .

The following screen will appear:

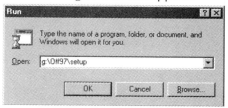

5 Type in the drive letter (A or D) followed by Setup. Don't forget the colon after the drive letter.

Note that it is a good idea, if you have enough room, to copy the Office 97 files from the CD onto a separate directory on your hard disk.

6 Just follow the on-screen instructions to install Office.

Note that you will need to make a note of the serial number and enter it during the installation procedure.

If you are unsure what to do at any of the Setup screens, press **OK** to accept the default settings.

Once Setup is complete, you can always run it again to install or remove components of Office.

Section 1
Word 97

Starting Word 97 for Windows

What you will learn in this unit

By the end of this unit you will be able to:

■ start Word 97

■ use Help

■ open an existing document

■ locate user directories and files

■ move around in a document

■ exit from Word 97.

Task 1: Starting Windows and Word

1   Switch on your computer. The Windows 95 screen should appear, similar to this one, with the Office toolbar displayed.

If your computer is on a network, for example at work or in a college, ask for details of any special log-on procedures, user IDs and passwords required.

If you still can't see Word, you probably need to install Office – see the 'Install and Start Office' section of your Office 97 manual.

If the Office toolbar doesn't appear, Office may not be installed properly on your computer.

2 If the Office toolbar is visible, as in this screen, click on the **File Open** button to start Word and open an existing document, or click the **New Document** button to start a new document. A screen similar to this one should appear:

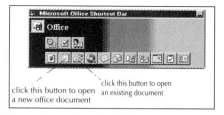

click this button to open a new office document

click this button to open an existing document

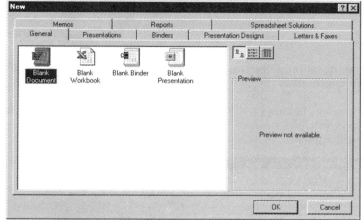

 Note: All instructions to click something mean press and release the left mouse button once only, unless otherwise stated.

3 If the Office toolbar is not visible, click and hold the left mouse button on the **Start** button at the bottom left of your screen, then while holding the left mouse button down, move the mouse up to Programs and across to the right to point to Microsoft Word, as in the screen on the right.

A screen similar to the one below will appear:

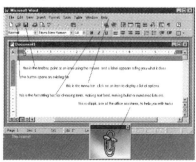

Task 2: Using Help

1   Click on the Help menu, then click
    on Microsoft Word Help. This
    screen should appear:

2   Type your question in the box, click **Search** , then click on one of the options
    for more information.

3   Close Help by clicking on the **Close** box, in the top right corner with an X in
    it. Click on **Help** Contents and index, then click on the **Index** tab. This
    screen will appear.

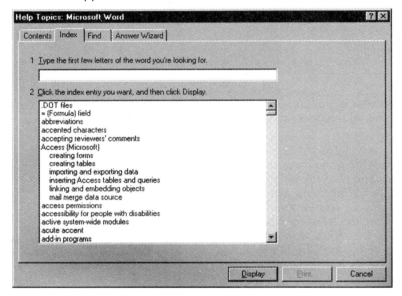

4   Type the first few letters to see help
    entries for those letters.

You can get a printout of any help topic
by clicking on the **Print** button. This
way you can build up your own set of
notes on using Word 97, tailored to
your own requirements.

On your own

Use Help and Clippit to revise the topics that we have covered so far. If there are
any that you want to print out, do so.

Task 3: Opening an existing document

1   Start Word 97 if it's not already running.

2   Click on the File menu and click on Open. The File Open dialog box should appear.

Dialog boxes are the windows that often appear in the middle of your screen when you use the menus.

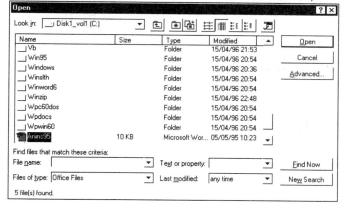

You can also click on the **Start** button, in the bottom left corner of your screen, then move the mouse to point to documents, then click on the document you want to open.

3   Click on the file that you want to open in the Files of type box (just below the File name box) then click on **Open**.

The file should now appear on your screen.

4   If the document is in another directory, click on the Look In box at the top of your screen, then click on Disk 1 (C) to show other directories.

If the document isn't visible it may be stored on another drive or directory. By default, only Word documents are shown in the list box.

Task 4: Moving through your document

1   Open any document. You can move the cursor in your text by using the arrow keys on the right-hand side of the keyboard. Try this now.

You get numbers 2, 4, 6 or 8 instead? The *Numlock* key and light is on. It's on the top right of your keyboard. Turn it off by pressing *Numlock* once and try again.

2   When you've got lots of text you can move the cursor more quickly by using the *PgUp* and *PgDn* keys to move up and down a screen at a time. Try this now.

3   You can also move the cursor with the mouse. Move the mouse pointer (an I-beam) to the location you want. Press and release the left mouse button once when the cursor is where you want it.

Your text has turned funny and is white on black (reverse video) as shown below? You were holding down the mouse button as you moved it. Move the mouse pointer to a blank bit of screen and click the left button once.

You can't move beyond your last line? That's because you're at the end of your document. Press the *Return* (*Enter*) key to move down a line.

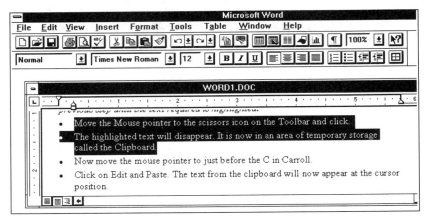

Your text turned funny as above then disappeared completely? Same as above plus you pressed another key while your text was highlighted. This deletes your text. Click on Edit on the menu bar and click on Undo Typing. Your text should be restored. Undo undoes the last thing you did. You can even undo an undo by clicking on Redo Typing!

Task 5: Moving around the screen

Practise moving the cursor using the mouse and the arrow keys.

Task 6: Moving to the beginning/end of your document

1   Hold down the *Ctrl* key and press *Home*. This moves you to the beginning of your document.

2   Hold down the *Ctrl* key and press *End*. This moves you to the end of your document.

Ctrl – Home didn't work, instead you got a Go To box like this?:

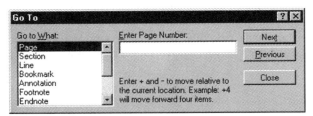

Type a 1 (one) in the Page Number box, then click **OK** and close. You should then be at the start.

The Go To box allows you to move straight to any page in your document, and is located on the Edit menu.

Task 7: Moving to a particular page in your document

1   You can move to anywhere in your document using the Edit menu. Drop down the Edit menu and click on Go To. When the dialog box appears type 1 (one) then click on **Go To** or press *Return*. You should go to the first page of your document. Type 2 to move to the second page, etc.

Task 8: Closing your document and exiting from Word

1   Click on File to drop down the File menu.

2   Click on Close.

                                                       If a dialog box like this one appears, click **No** .

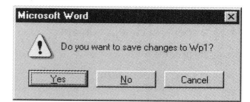

Your document will then be closed for you.

3   To exit from Word, click File, then Exit.

Starting a new document

What you will learn in this unit

By the end of this unit you will be able to:

- enter text
- insert text
- delete text
- spell-check a document
- replace text
- save a document.

Entering text

As soon as the Word screen appears, you can start typing your text. You can also open a new document over an existing one.

Task 1: Entering text

1 Click File, New and click **OK** in the New dialog box.

The New dialog box lets you select templates for different styles of letter, memo, fax etc.

2 Type in the following text; don't press *Return* (*Enter*) at the end of the line. Word wrap will automatically move you onto the next line.

> Carroll and his colleagues have been among the first to recognise that users should develop skills both for doing things (i.e. constructive skills) and for undoing things that have gone wrong (i.e. corrective skills). Being able to detect, diagnose and correct errors is an important skill for all users who need to master a computer program. The provision of error information is therefore a key feature of the Minimalist Manual approach.

If you get a gap in your text like this:

> Carroll and his colleagues have been
>
> among the first to recognise that users should develop skills both for doing things (i.e. constructive skills) and for undoing things that have gone

it's because you accidentally hit return after been. You can correct this by moving the cursor to just before the a in among then pressing the *Backspace* key.

Task 2: Starting a new paragraph

1   After the last word, 'approach', in the text you have just typed, press the *Return* key. The cursor moves down one line to allow you to begin a new paragraph. Now type in the following text:

Studies have shown that using the Minimalist Manual approach reduces learning time, reduces the size of the manual and improves user performance.

Correcting text

Word 97 automatically monitors your spelling as you type. Any word that appears to be misspelt is underlined with a red wavy line on screen.

Task 3: Correcting spelling

1   To correct spelling, move the mouse pointer to the underlined word and click the right mouse button to display a list of possible corrections, as in this screen:

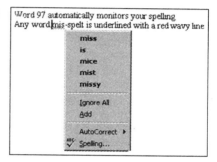

2   Click on the correct word from the list, or choose Ignore All if the word is correct.

The Add option adds the word to the Word dictionary. This is useful for unusual words, proper names etc.

Task 4: Correcting text

1   Type the word recognize.

2   Place the cursor just after the 'z' and press the *Backspace* key once (the key to the right of the + and = key).

3   Now type the letter s.

If the 'e' in recognise disappears when you type the letter s it's because Ins is on. On the right of your keyboard there is an *Ins* key. It acts like a switch to turn overtype mode on and off. Press the *Ins* key once only, then retype the missing e.

4   Move to the letter 's' in recognise and press the *Delete* key. Now type a z.

5   Go to somewhere in the text you've just typed and practise using the *Backspace* key to delete some text. Now use the *Delete* key. Can you see the difference between the way they work?

Task 5: Using overtype/overwrite mode

1   Sometimes, it is useful to use over-type mode. Type in the following text (it's supposed to be entered twice):

Go to somewhere in the text you've just typed and practise using the back-space key to

Go to somewhere in the text you've just typed and practise using the back-space key to

2   Now press and release the *Ins* key on the lower right of your keyboard. The **OVR** button on the Word status bar at the bottom of the screen should change from grey to black. Check it now.

If the button is still grey, you were probably already in overtype mode. Just press it once more.

3   Now move the cursor to the begin-ning of 'Go' on the third line. Type in the following:

Inserting text with OVR on deletes the text after the insertion point.

Most of the third line has now been replaced with the text above.

Task 6: Moving to a new page

1   Force Word 97 to move to a new page, by holding down the *Ctrl* key and pressing *Return*. This is called a page break.

2   You can delete a page break by moving the cursor to the new page and pressing the *Backspace* key. Practise this now.

You can also insert a page break by dropping down the Insert menu, clicking Break, Page Break and **OK**.

Task 7: Saving your work

1 Click on the File menu on the menu bar. This screen should appear.

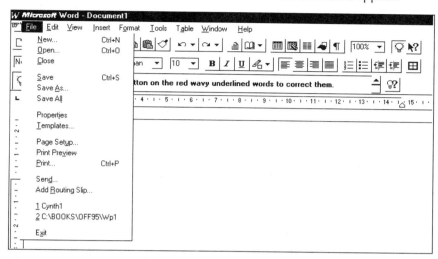

If an Open window appears instead, it's because you clicked on the **File Open** icon on the toolbar. Click on **Cancel** , then make sure the mouse pointer is in the middle of the word File on the menu bar.

2 Click on Save as. This window should appear (it won't be exactly the same).

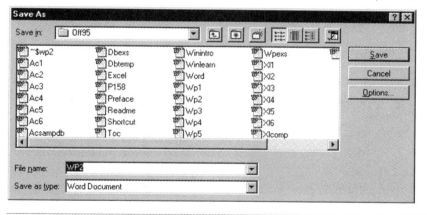

3 Move the cursor to the File name box and type: My first Word document

The name **My first Word document** will appear in the File name window

File names are limited to a maximum of 255 characters with spaces, numbers and full stops also allowed as well as letters.

Note that if you want to use your file with other older word processors, or with Word 6, filenames should be limited to a maximum of eight characters with no spaces or punctuation, followed by a three-character extension (.doc).

| 4 | Click the **Save** button in the top right of the box. | A message will appear in the status bar (at the bottom left of your screen) telling you that Word is saving your work. The message may be too quick to actually read. |

Congratulations! You've now successfully created your first Word document (file).

The File menu

Use this for opening new or existing documents, saving your work, previewing and printing, setting up pages, closing documents, exiting from Word etc.

New is for starting a new empty file.

Open is for opening an existing file. It's easy to confuse these two.

Save is for the second and successive times that you save a file.

Save As is for the first time you save a file.

Spell-checking your work and replacing text

In addition to Word's on-line spell-checking, Word can also check your finished document. You may prefer to ignore the on-line spell-checking, and wait until the end of your document.

Task 8: Spell-checking a finished document

1 Open **My first Word document** if it's not already open.

| 2 | Click on the Tools menu and click on Spelling. A screen similar to the following should appear:  | Not all words that appear in the Not in Dictionary box are spelling mistakes, e.g. proper names. Also note that the US English dictionary may be installed, which will use US Spellings. To change the dictionary, drop down the Tools menu, click Language, Set Language and choose the desired dictionary. |

3 If you want to accept the suggested word, click on **Change** . If not, click **Ignore** .

| 4 | Save your work when the spell-check is complete, so that the corrections are saved. | You should always spell-check your work, regardless of how good a speller you are, since it is very easy to transpose letters such as *teh* instead of *the*. In fact, Word 97 will automatically correct this particular mistake. |

Task 9: Finding and replacing text

1 Click on Edit, Replace. This box appears.

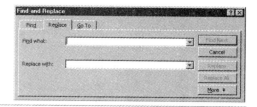

2 In the Find What box type the.

3 Move to the Replace With box either with the mouse pointer or the *Tab* key.

4 In the Replace With box type: ravioli.

5 Click on **Replace All** . A dialog box will ask if you want to search the rest of the document. Say **Yes** . All the's should now read ravioli.

Changed your mind? Click on Edit, Undo Replace to undo the operation.

Exiting from Word

Task 10: Exiting from Word

1 Click on the File menu.

2 Click on Exit. A box will ask if you want to save changes to your work. Click on **Yes** to save changes. You will be returned to the Windows main screen.

3 To exit from Windows 95, click on the **Start** button in the bottom left corner of your screen, then click on Shut Down, then click **Yes** . Wait until a message appears telling you that it's safe to turn your computer off.

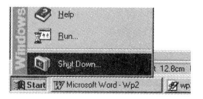

Working with documents on floppy disks

Task 11: Opening a document on a floppy disk

1 Start Word 97 if it's not already running.

2 Insert a floppy disk with some Word files on it into the disk drive.

3   Click on File, Open. This dialog box will appear.

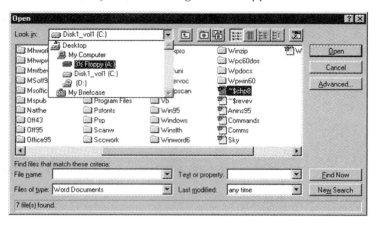

4   Click on the arrow to the right of the Look in box.

5   Click on the 3½ Floppy (A) drive symbol on the left of the box.

The Drives and Directories boxes should change to Drive A. A list of your files with the .doc Word extension (if there are any) will appear in the File name box.

6   Click on the file you want to open then click **Open**.

Drive A: not visible in the box? This is most likely to happen on a network. You need to click on the scroll arrow to the left of the Drives box until Drive A: appears.

Your file name doesn't appear in the File name box? This is most likely because you gave it an extension other than .doc or it's a different kind of file, for example an Excel file. By default Word only shows files with the .doc extension. To show other types of file, click on the Files of Type box arrow and click on All Files.

Task 12: Saving a document to floppy disk

1   Click on File, then Open, then click on My first Word document.

2   Insert a formatted floppy disk in Drive A:.

Make sure the label side is facing up and the metal slide is facing towards the drive. Push in firmly until it clicks into place.

3   Click on File, Save As.

4   Click on the arrow to the right of the Save In box.

5   Click on the 3½ Floppy (A:) icon then click on Save. The file will be saved on Drive A:.

If you can't get the drive to change to A:, it's probably because your disk is either write protected or hasn't been formatted. Ask your support technician or tutor to check this for you.

Task 13: On your own

1   Now practise opening files on your network or drive C: and using the File, Save As command to save them on drive A:.

2   Practise opening files on Drive A:.

You can't save your file? It's very easy to accidentally click on the File open icon which is just below the File menu, with the result that the Open dialog box is displayed instead of the Save As box. As these two boxes are virtually identical, it's necessary to read the heading in the box's menu bar. If it's the wrong box, click on **Cancel** and start again.

Text and document layout and formatting

What you will learn in this unit

By the end of this unit you will be able to:

- embolden, underline text, use italics
- change margins
- alter line spacing
- set page size
- use justification controls, centre text
- indent paragraphs, use hanging indents
- tabulate lines of text
- choose and change appropriate fonts
- insert page numbers
- work with tables.

Text enhancement: bold, underline and italics

You can make text stand out by emboldening, underlining or italicising it. Use bold in preference to underlining, and only use italics for short passages, not for a whole document, as it's harder to read.

Task 1: Enhancing text

1 Open a Word document.

2 Select the first line in your document.	A useful shortcut is to move the mouse pointer into the left margin and click once. The whole line should be highlighted. Practise this now.
3 Move the Mouse pointer to the **B** button on the toolbar and click once.	Notice how the **B** button looks as though its been pressed compared to the other buttons.

4   Move the mouse pointer outside your text and click to release the highlighting. Your text will now appear in bold.

Nothing seems to have happened? You can only tell if your text is bold when the highlighting is off. If there's still a problem, you probably didn't select your text before clicking on the **Bold** button.

Task 2: On your own

Now try the *Italics* and **Underlining** buttons, next to the **Bold** button on the toolbar. You use them in the same way as bold.

When you carry on typing, your new text is bold /italicised /underlined? You need to click once more on the relevant button to turn off the text enhancement.

Task 3: Undoing text enhancement

1   Select a portion of your text that is in bold.

2   Click on the **B** button, then release the highlighting. Your text should revert to normal.

If this hasn't worked, repeat the procedure.

Text alignment and justification

Task 4: Centring and justifying text

1   Select a paragraph from your document with the mouse by double clicking in the left margin.

2   Click on the **Centre** button on the toolbar. Your text will be centred. Centring is useful for headings, menus etc.

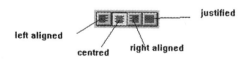

left aligned

centred   right aligned

justified

Task 5: On your own

Now practise right aligning and justifying your text using the buttons on the toolbar. Left alignment is the default setting.

Don't use justification unless you are told to, as it can cause problems with layout and is now considered rather out of date.

Indenting text

Task 6: Indenting text

1   Select a paragraph with the mouse.

2   Click on the **Right (increase) Indent** button on the toolbar. Don't confuse the right indent button with the right aligned button.

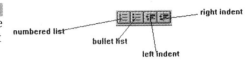

numbered list

bullet list

right indent

left indent

3   Leave the highlighting on and click once more on the **Right Indent** button.

4   Click once on the **Left Indent** button. Your text should now be indented by one Tab stop. Each time you click, the paragraph is moved one tab stop.

For more help on text alignment, use Word's Help, Index option. You may want to do this now and get a printout of the topic.

Task 7: Indenting text with tabs

1   Type your name and address as you would at the head of a letter, but aligned with the left margin e.g.

    S.P. Bloggs

    10 Serf Close

    Nastytown

    CEF1 6YU

2   Move the cursor to the start of each line and press the *Tab* key. Just as with the right indent button, your text will move right. How much it moves will depend on the tab settings, which you can change in the Format, Tabs menu.

3   Repeat for each line of your address.

Your text disappeared when you hit the *Tab* key? You highlighted it instead of placing the cursor before it. Click Edit, Undo to get it back.

Whenever you want to arrange text in columns, for example in a Curriculum vitae section listing qualifications with dates obtained in two columns, you should use tabs. The default tab setting is 0.5" or 1 cm per tab, but you can change this. 1" equals 2.5 cm

(!)   **Never** use spaces instead of tabs, because although it may look okay on screen it will cause big problems when you try to print out your work.

The United States and older adults use inches rather than centimetres.

Task 8: On your own

Type a list in two columns of your qualifications and dates obtained.

Numbered and bulleted lists

Task 9: Creating lists

1   Type in the following, exactly as shown:

>   Turn alarm off
>
>   Get out of bed
>
>   Put coffee on
>
>   Return to bed with coffee and paper.

2   Select the above text with the mouse.

3   Click on the **Numbered List** button on the toolbar.

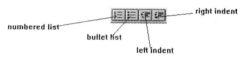

4   Move out of the text and click to release the highlighting.

Your text should now look like this:

1. Turn alarm off

2. Get out of bed

3. Put coffee on

4. Return to bed with coffee and paper.

5   Now re-select the text.

Click the **Bulleted List** button on the toolbar. The numbers should be replaced with bullets.

Headers and footers

Placing your filename in the footer makes it much easier to find your work in the future.

Task 10: Placing your filename in a footer

1   Click on View, Header/Footer. This screen appears.

2 Click on the **Switch Between Header and Footer** button. This takes you into the footer area.

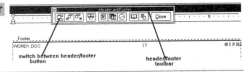

3 Click the arrowhead to the right of Insert AutoText. This menu appears.

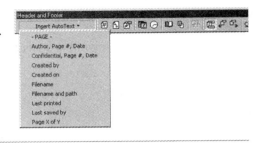

4 Click Filename to insert the filename in the footer.

5 Click **Close** to return to your document.

Setting and changing margins

Task 11: Changing margins

1 Click File, Page Setup. This dialog box will appear.

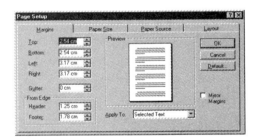

2 Change top and bottom margins to 10cm and left and right to 7cm. Use the mouse to move to each box, and click **OK** .

Margins are in inches? You can choose to work in inches or cms by going to the Settings option from the **Start** button, choosing Control Panel, then choosing Regional Settings. Traditionally, the printing and publishing industries work in inches rather than centimetres.

Setting and changing line spacing

Task 12: Changing line spacing

1   Click on Format, Paragraph to display this dialog box.

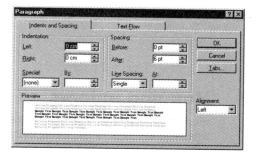

2   Click on the **down arrow** in the Line Spacing box.

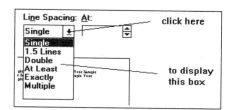

3   Click on Double, then on **OK** to set line spacing to double.

Setting and changing page size and layout

Task 13: Changing paper size

1   Click File, Page Setup. The Page Setup dialog box will appear.

2   Click the **Paper Size** tab. This box will appear.

Two paper sizes are in common use, A4 in Europe, and US letter, which is slightly wider and shorter, in the US. Note that the US uses inches rather than the metric system.

3   Click the **down arrow** in the Paper size box to drop the box down.

4   Click on the paper size required, then click **OK** .

You will need to check what paper size you are using. Selecting the wrong paper size can stop your printer working – you may see a message on the printer saying 'Load Letter', which means that paper size is set for US letter 8½ by 11 in. paper. If so, check your paper size and setting.

Hanging indents

Hanging indents are used automatically when you use bullet points or numbered lists. The first line of the paragraph 'hangs out' to the left of the main body text on second and subsequent lines, like in the example below:

This is an example of the use of hanging indents. The first line of the paragraph extends further to the left than subsequent lines. In this example, the indent is set to 0.5".

Task 14: Setting a hanging indent

1   Open a Word file of your choice.

2   Select the text that you want to indent.

3   Drop down the **Format** menu and click on **Paragraph** to display this box.

4   In the **Special** box, click on the **down arrow** to drop down the options and click **Hanging**.

5   The default indent is 0.5" (it may be different on your system). If this is okay, click on **OK** to set the hanging indent. Otherwise, you can choose a different value.

Note that the preview box gives you an impression of how your text will look.

In the above task, the first line is lined up with the body text by specifying 0" in the **Left indentation** field of the **Paragraph** box. This is the default setting, but you can change this to other values.

Task 15: Setting a hanging indent and indenting text

1 To indent text by 1.0″, with a first line indent of 0.5″, select the paragraph to be indented.

2 Click on Format, Paragraph.

3 Drop down the Special choices and click on Hanging.

4 Set the Left indentation field to 0.5″.

Your text will appear as below:

> *In the above example, the first line is lined up with the body text by specifying 0″ in the Left indentation field of the Paragraph box. This is the default.*

Choosing and changing fonts in Word

Fonts and typefaces

 Typeface is the name given to the set of letters of the alphabet etc. in a particular style, such as Arial or Times New Roman. A font is a particular combination of typeface and size, e.g. Arial normal 10-point. However, in practice the terms font and typeface are often used interchangeably, with people referring to the Arial font etc.

Fonts today are usually proportional, with less space being allocated for 'thin' letters like 'i' and 'n' compared with m and w. However, older non-proportional fonts allocated the same amount of space for all letters.

Research has shown that for body text (the main body of reports, articles etc.) proportional serif fonts (with little 'tails' on the end of the letters r, l, t etc.) such as Times New Roman, in 10 to 12-point, are the most readable. This paragraph is written in Times New Roman, a proportional serif font. The Times family of fonts are all proportional serif fonts and are available with Windows 95 and most printers. Examples of other serif fonts include Palatino, Bookman, and New Century Schoolbook. As a general rule don't use more than two fonts on a page; instead make use of different sizes of the same font, and text enhancement facilities such as bold and italics.

Font size

 Font size is traditionally measured in points, with 72 points to one inch (the typesetting industry traditionally uses inches). The larger the point size, the larger the print. Older, non-proportional fonts such as Elite and Courier are measured in cpi (characters per inch), with higher cpi values giving smaller print. However, it is unusual to find non-proportional fonts in use now.

Fonts for headings, footnotes, captions

Sans serif fonts such as Helvetica, Arial and Univers lack the little feet and tails of serif fonts, and can make lines of text harder to read, so they are less often used for body text. They are best used for short pieces of text. Spreadsheets such as Excel use sans serif fonts for cell contents and chart labels. Headings, captions and footnotes are all suitable for sans serif fonts. This paragraph has been written in Arial 12-point, a sans serif font, so that you can compare serif and sans serif fonts.

For captions on charts, footnotes etc. a smaller point size such as 8-point is usually suitable. These last two sentences have been written in 8 point.

As a general rule, when working on Windows systems, choose Times New Roman for body text and Arial for headings, etc., unless you particularly want to use other fonts.

Task 16: Changing font

1   Select the text you wish to change with the mouse.

2   Click on the **arrow** in the Font box to drop down the list of available fonts.

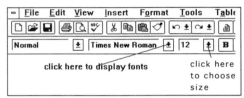

3   Scroll through the list and select the desired font.

4   Drop down the Font Size box and type in or click on the desired size. The font will adjust to the desired size.

Page numbering

Task 17: Inserting page numbers

1   Open a new document.

2   Drop down the Insert menu and click on Page Numbers. This box will appear.

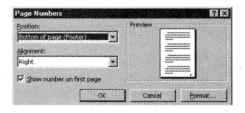

3   Click on the **down arrow** in the Position box if you wish to place the page number at the top of the page (header). The default setting is in the footer.

4   Use the Alignment box to position the page number in the centre, left, or right of the footer (or header).

5   If you don't want a page number on the first page, for example on the cover of a report, click on the Show Number on First Page box so that it is blank.

6   To start page numbering at a partic-
    ular page (other than the first page,
    for example if you have a cover
    sheet but want numbering to start
    with page one from the first page
    after the cover), click on **Format** in
    the Page Numbers box to display
    this box.

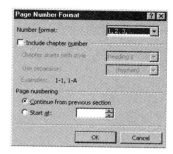

7   Click on the **Start At** button and enter the page number of the first page for
    numbering.

8   You may also include chapter and   For more information on page
    page numbers, e.g. II–4 to indicate   numbering, use Help.
    the fourth page of Chapter II, etc.

On your own

Experiment with some of the different page numbering options with a document
of your own.

Tables

You can use tables to lay text out in cells, similar to a spreadsheet, with or without
gridlines. One example of the use of tables might be when constructing a CV
(Curriculum vitae), where it is usual to line up rows and columns of information
such as exam results and dates, etc. Although you can do this kind of layout with
tabs, it is sometimes easier to use a table, particularly if the text is several lines
long.

Task 18: Using tables to construct a CV

1   Type the text in the box below, inserting one tab stop after **Subject**, **Grade** and
    Date.

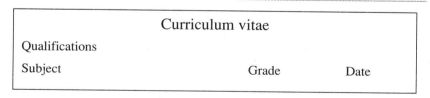

2   Select the line beginning 'Subject...'

3   Drop down the Table menu.

4 Click Convert Text to Table. This box is displayed.

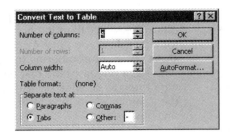

5 Click Tabs in the Separate Text At section then click **OK** . A dotted border will appear around your text, as in this screen shot.

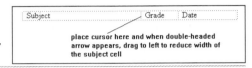

6 Adjust the size of the 'Subject' cell by dragging the cell border.

7 Place the cursor at the end of the word 'Date' and press the *Tab* key once. A new row will appear. Fill in details of your qualifications, listing each on a separate row. If necessary, adjust the width of the cells.

8 When you have entered all your subjects, select the whole table, drop down the Format menu, click Borders and Shading, then click Grid to surround your table with gridlines.

Task 19: On your own

1 Add new rows, columns or cells by placing the cursor in a cell and dropping down the Table menu, then click Insert Cells (or rows/columns).

2 Use similar procedures to step 1 to delete rows/columns/cells from the Table menu. Cut or Copy a cell, row or column, and Paste it to another location.

3 Clear the contents of a cell, without deleting it, by selecting the text and pressing the *Delete* key.

4 Make columns equal in width, by dropping down the Table menu and clicking Distribute Columns Evenly.

5 The Table menu also contains an option to sort rows.

Moving and copying blocks of text

What you will learn in this unit

By the end of this unit you will be able to:

■ move text

■ copy text

■ replace words.

Moving text with the clipboard

Task 1: Using the clipboard

1 Open **My first word document**.

> You can use any other Word document instead, but you will have to modify the following instructions.

2 Move the mouse pointer to just before the 'B' of 'Being' on the third line.

3 Hold down the left mouse button and, while keeping it held, move the cursor down until the rest of the document is highlighted in reverse video (white on black), rather like in this screen.

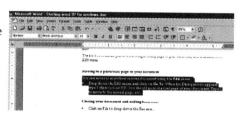

> Too much or the wrong text highlighted? Click the left mouse button and repeat the previous steps until the required text is highlighted.

4 Move the mouse pointer to the scissors icon on the toolbar and cut the highlighted text by clicking the icon.

> The highlighted text will disappear. It is now in an area of temporary storage called the clipboard.

5 Now move the mouse pointer to just to the left of the 'C' in 'Carroll' (or any other position in your document).

6 Click on the Edit menu and Paste. The text from the clipboard will now appear at the cursor position.

Cutting text deletes it from your document and stores it on the Windows clipboard. You can also cut text using the Edit menu.

You can use the same method, called Cutting and Pasting, to move any text. The clipboard will only hold one selection of text at a time; selecting another piece of text and cutting it to the clipboard will delete the first text from the clipboard. You can even use this method to move text from one document to another, or to move text from a wordprocessor to a database, spreadsheet or most other Windows applications.

Selecting whole words and whole paragraphs

To select just one word, a useful shortcut is to move the mouse pointer onto the word and double-click. The whole word will be highlighted. To select the whole paragraph, move the mouse to anywhere in the paragraph and triple click. You can undo the selection by clicking once.

Moving text with drag and drop

Task 2: Dragging and dropping text

1 Move the mouse pointer to the 'B' of 'Being' again and select the rest of that sentence.

2 Move the mouse pointer below the highlighted text and up slightly until a backwards sloping white pointer appears.

3 Hold down the left mouse button. A small grey square will appear under the mouse pointer. Keep holding the mouse button.

4 Still holding down the button, drag the mouse until the grey vertical bar above the pointer is just after the full stop after (i.e. corrective skills).

5 Release the button. The highlighted sentence will move to the mouse cursor position.

Your text ended up in the wrong place? Click on Edit, Undo then try again. You can also click the **Undo** button on the toolbar.

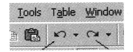

Your text ended up in the wrong place, but you couldn't use undo? Select the text again and try dragging and dropping it in the right location.

Drag and drop is just another way of moving text. With practice, it is faster than using the Clipboard. However, you do need to spend some time practising as it's all too easy to let go of the mouse button in the wrong place. Practise it now.

Copying text

Moving text deletes the text from its original location and places it somewhere else. Copying is when you leave the original text in place and make a copy of it somewhere else.

Task 3: Copying text

1 Select the entire text in your document (Edit, Select All).

2 Click on Edit, Copy. A copy is placed in the clipboard.

3 Move the mouse cursor to the end of your text (*Ctrl–end*).

4 Click on Edit, Paste. Another copy of your text will appear after the first.   You can undo a copy using Edit, Undo.

You can paste as many copies of your text as you like. Anything in the clipboard remains there until something else is cut or copied to the clipboard. So if you have to type the same word or phrase over and over again in a document you can copy it to the clipboard and use paste instead of retyping it.

On your own

Now practise moving and copying text using both the clipboard and drag and drop.

Copying text to a new document

Task 4: Copying text to a new document

1 Select some text and copy it to the clipboard.

2 Click on File, New and open a new document.

3 Click on File, Paste. Your text should appear in the new document.

4 Click on File, Close to close the new document (don't bother saving it) and return to the original.

Printing your work

What you will learn in this unit

By the end of this unit you will be able to:

■ produce printed copies of complete documents

■ use templates and wizards to produce documents.

Previewing and printing

Task 1: Preview and print document

1   Click on the File menu and click on Print Preview.

A screen similar to the one below should appear:

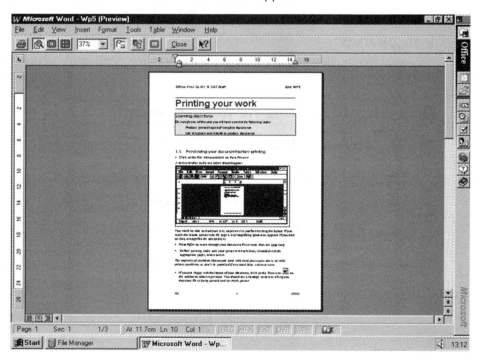

You won't be able to read your text, as preview is just for checking the layout.
If you move the mouse pointer into the page a tiny magnifying glass icon
appears. If you click on this, it magnifies the selected text.

2 Press *PgDn* to move through your document if it is more than one page long.

Before printing, make sure your printer is switched on, is loaded with the appropriate paper, and is on-line.

The majority of problems that people have with word processors are to do with printer problems, so don't be surprised if you need help. If you can't get your printer to work, you may need to contact the supplier or manufacturer for a new printer driver.

3 If you are happy with the layout of your document, click on the **Print** icon on the toolbar to obtain a printout. You should see a message on screen telling you that your file is being prepared for printing.

4 If you need to make changes before printing, click the **Close** button to return to your document.

You should always preview your documents before printing.

Your printer flashes a message such as 'Load letter'? This is because you are either out of paper, or the wrong paper size has been chosen in the Page Setup. To change paper size, go back to the section on page size and layout.

You get a 'Paper jam' message or other message? Check to see if some paper is caught in your printer.

Business letter templates: layout and style

You may be required to use a 'house style' for laying out letters or other documents. Check with your organisation if this is the case. You may be instructed to set fonts, margins, line spacing, etc. yourself, using the Setup commands above, or to load a particular file that is already formatted for you. Word comes with several 'Wizards' and templates to help you create documents with an appropriate style.

Task 2: Using a template

1 Click on File, New then click the **Letters & Faxes** tab to display this screen.

2 Click on one of the choices to display a preview of the layout for that template.

3 Click **OK** to create your letter or
   other document. A document will
   be displayed with instructions telling
   you what to type and where, as in
   this screen.

 Wizards are step-by-step guides to producing standard documents. Practise using
a wizard now on your own.

Section 2
Excel 97

Introduction to Excel 97

What you will learn in this unit

By the end of this unit you will be able to:

- start Excel
- locate user directories and files
- exit from Excel
- retrieve a spreadsheet from disk.

Note that this unit uses the Samples workbook from the Excel/Examples sub-directory. In case this has not been installed on your system, it is printed at the end of this unit.

Introduction to spreadsheets

Spreadsheets such as Excel are used for dealing with data that is largely numerical rather than textual (although they can deal with both types of data). They can be thought of as the equivalent of a word processor for dealing with numeric data and calculations. In business and other organisations they are most commonly used for the preparation of budgets, cash-flow forecasts and 'What-if' analysis, where a company might use a spreadsheet to model the effect of, for example, a 20 percent increase in demand for its products, or a change in the rate of VAT etc.

The term spreadsheet is used both to refer to software packages such as Lotus 123, Excel, Supercalc, Quattro, etc., and also to refer to an individual spreadsheet, worksheet or workbook, which is a grid of cells made up of columns across the screen and rows going down the screen.

Worksheets are often larger than the computer screen, so the screen becomes a window (not to be confused with Microsoft Windows, a software operating environment) onto part of the worksheet. In Excel, a group of one or more related worksheets are called a workbook. When this book refers to creating, opening, saving, etc. a workbook, it is referring to what other packages may call a spreadsheet or worksheet.

The maximum size of an Excel 97 worksheet is 256 columns labelled A, B, C and so on, and 65,536 rows labelled row 1, 2, 3 and so on. Each cell on a worksheet has a unique reference given by its column letter and row number, as in C5, AF345, G67 etc., and can contain up to 32,000 characters.

Starting Excel

Task 1: Starting Excel

1   Switch on your computer and click on the **Start** button at the bottom left of the screen.

2   Move the mouse pointer to Programs, then across to Microsoft Excel, then click on Excel as shown in this screen.

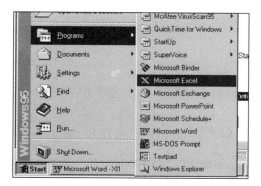

You will notice that Excel is added to the **Taskbar** at the bottom of the screen:

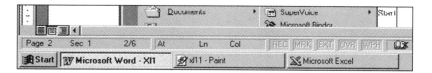

When you open Excel a screen similar to this one will appear.

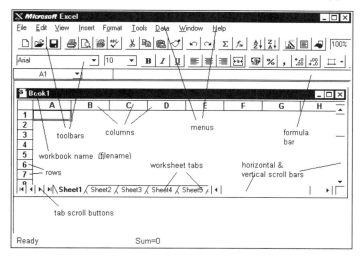

Using Help

Task 2: Using Help

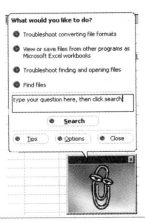

1 Click on the Help menu, then click on Microsoft Excel Help. This screen should appear.

2 Type your question in the box, click **Search** then click on the topic that best matches your question.

3 Close Help by clicking on the **Close** box, in the top right corner with an X in it.

4 Click on Help, Contents and Index, then click on the **Index** tab. The following screen will appear:

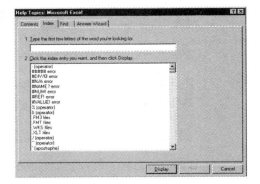

5 Type the first few letters to see help entries for those letters.

 You can get a printout of any help topic by selecting it, clicking on File in the Help box, then clicking on Print Topic. This way you can build up your own set of notes on using Excel 97, tailored to your own requirements. Pressing *F1* will also display the What would you like to do? box.

On your own

Use Help to look at the topic saving files. If you want to print out a topic, do so.

Opening an existing workbook

Task 3: Open a workbook

1 Start Excel if it's not already running.

Excel calls each individual spreadsheet a workbook, which may be made up of one or more worksheets. For the purposes of this book, the terms worksheet, workbook and spreadsheet can be used interchangeably.

2 Click on the File menu and click on Open. The Open dialog box should appear.

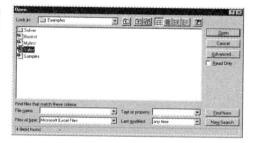

3 Click on the **arrow** next to the Look in box to display the Examples folder (directory) in the MS Office/Excel folder.

4 Click on **Samples.xls**, then click on **Open**. Double-click **Enable macros** then click the **Source** tab to display this worksheet.

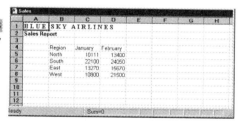

If the document isn't visible it may be stored on another drive or directory. You can ignore the boxes about macros and visual basic, as they are for more advanced users.

Closing your workbook and exiting from Excel

Task 4: Closing your workbook

1 Click on File to drop down the File menu, then click Close to close your workbook.

2 Click on File to drop down the File menu, then click Exit to leave Excel and return to the opening screen.

You may see a box asking you if you want to save changes to your work. Click **No** if this box is displayed.

Appendix: The Sales.xls workbook from the Excel/examples sub-directory

If this file is not available on your system, you can quickly type in the data as shown below.

	A	B	C	D
1	B L U E S K Y A I R L I N E S			
2	*Sales Report*			
3				
4		Region	January	February
5		North	10111	13400
6		South	22100	24050
7		East	13270	15670
8		West	10800	21500

Opening and using
a workbook

What you will learn in this unit

By the end of this unit you will be able to:

- locate user directories and files
- retrieve a workbook from disk
- move the cell pointer to any cell in the workbook
- save a workbook.

Moving the cursor

Task 1: Moving around the workbook

1 If it's not already open, open the Samples workbook that you used in the last unit. Remember to click the **Source** tab.

2 Move the cursor in your worksheet by using the _arrow keys_ on the right-hand side of the keyboard. Try this now to display the Sales Report data. | If you get numbers 2, 4, 6 or 8 instead and the _Numlock_ key and light is on (it's on the top right of your keyboard), turn it off by pressing _Numlock_ once and try again.

3 When you've got lots of rows of data you can move the cursor more quickly by using the _PgUp_ and _PgDn_ keys to move up and down a screen at a time. Try this now.

4 To move one screen to the right, press the _Alt_ key and _PgDn_ key together.

5 To move one screen to the left, press _Alt_ and _PgUp_ keys together.

6 To move further to the right, just keep pressing the _right arrow_ key.

7 To move back to cell A1, press the _Ctrl_ and _Home_ keys together.

8 Pressing the _Home_ key on its own takes you back to column A.

9 To move to the last column, (IV) press the _Ctrl_ and _right arrow_ keys together.

10 To move to the last cell containing data, press _Ctrl_ and _End_ keys together.

11 To move to the last row (65,536), press _Ctrl_ and the _down arrow_ keys together.

12 You can also move the cursor with the mouse. Move the mouse pointer (a big white plus sign) to the location you want. Press and release the left mouse button once when the cursor is where you want it.

13 Another way to move around is to use the horizontal and vertical scroll bars with the mouse. The screen shot below shows the scroll bars. To move down your workbook, place the mouse pointer on the vertical scroll bar **down arrow** and click until you reach the desired position. To move up, click on the **up arrow**. To move to the right, use the **right arrow** in the horizontal scroll bar, and the **left arrow** to move left. Practise this now.

The Excel 97 screen

	A	B	C	D	E	F	
1	BLUE SKY AIRLINES						
2	Sales Report						
3							
4		Region	January	February			
5		North	10111	13400			
6		South	22100	24050			
7		East	13270	15670			
8		West	10800	21500			
9							

Sales Report / Sheet2 / Sheet3 / S

If your text has turned funny and is white on black (reverse video), you were holding down the mouse button as you moved it. Move the mouse pointer to a blank bit of screen and click the left button once.

Task 2: Moving to a particular cell

1 Click on the Edit menu, choose Go To; this window appears.

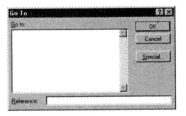

2 Enter the cell reference of the cell you want to go to. It doesn't matter whether you use upper or lower case.

3 Click on **OK** to move directly to the chosen cell. With a small worksheet, just use the mouse and click on the required cell.

On your own

Practise moving the cursor using the mouse and the *arrow* keys as instructed above.

How many cells can an Excel 97 worksheet contain?

Saving your work

Task 3: Saving a workbook

1 Click on the File menu on the Menu bar.

2   Click on Save As. This window should appear (it may not be exactly the same).

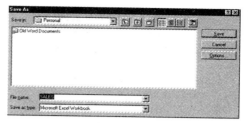

If an Open window appears instead, it's because you clicked on the **File Open** icon on the toolbar. Click on **Cancel** then make sure the mouse pointer is in the middle of the word File on the menu bar.

3   Move the cursor to the beginning of the File name box and click once. Delete any name that is already there and type the name My First Workbook.

The name **My First Workbook** will appear in the File name window.

File names are limited to a maximum of 255 characters with spaces, numbers and full stops allowed, but if you are going to be using your workbook with older versions of Excel, such as Excel 5, or other spreadsheet packages, you should use file names of eight characters with no spaces or punctuation followed by a three-character extension (.xls).

4   Then click the **Save** button in the top right of the box.

Congratulations! You've now successfully created your first Excel workbook (file).

The File menu

Use this for opening new or existing documents, saving your work, previewing and printing, setting up pages, closing documents, exiting from Excel, etc.

■ Home is for starting a new empty file

■ Open is for opening an existing file. It's easy to confuse these two

■ Save is for the second and successive times that you save a file

■ Save As is for the first time you save a file.

You can also save worksheets as World Wide Web pages or send them via email from the File menu.

Exiting from Excel

Task 4: Exiting from Excel

1 Click on the File menu. This screen will appear.

2 Click on Exit. A box will ask if you want to save changes to your work. Click on **OK** to save changes. You will be returned to the Windows main screen.

3 To exit from Windows 95, click on the **Start** button in the bottom left corner of your screen, then click on Shut Down, then click **Yes**. Wait until a message appears telling you that it's safe to turn your computer off.

Working with floppy disks

Task 5: Opening a workbook on a floppy disk

1 Start Excel 97 if it's not already running.

2 Insert a floppy disk with some Excel files on it into the disk drive.

3 Click on File, Open. This dialog box will appear.

4 Click on the **down arrow** to the right of the Look in box. A list of drives will appear.

5 Click on the 3½ Floppy (A:) drive symbol on the left of the box. The Open box should change to Drive A:.

A list of your Excel files (if there are any) will appear in the file name box.

6 Click on the file you want to open then click Open.

Drive A: not visible in the box? This is most likely to happen on a network. You need to click on the **scroll arrow** to the left of the Drives box until Drive A: appears.

Your file name doesn't appear in the File name box? This is most likely because you gave it an extension other than .xls or it's a different kind of file, for example a Word file. By default Excel only shows files with the .xls extension. To show other types of file, click on the Files of Type box arrow and click on All Files.

Task 6: Saving a workbook to floppy disk

1 Open the Sales report **(samples.xls)** file used earlier (or any other file) on Drive C: or your network drive.

2 Insert a formatted floppy disk in Drive A:.

Make sure the label side is facing up and the metal slide is facing towards the drive. Push in firmly until it clicks into place.

3 Click on File, Save As.

4 Click on the **arrow** in the Save in box.

5 Click on the 3½ Floppy (A:) icon then click on **Save** . The file will be saved on Drive A: with the name **samples.xls**.

If you can't get the drive to change to A: it's probably because your disk is either write protected or hasn't been formatted. Click the **Start** button, Help and type formatting disks for help on disk formatting.

On your own

Now practise opening files on your network or Drive C: and using the File Save As command to save them on Drive A:.

Practise opening files on Drive A:.

 You can't save your file? It's very easy to accidentally click on the **File** open icon which is just below the File menu, with the result that the Open dialog box is displayed instead of the Save As box. As these two boxes are virtually identical, it's necessary to read the heading in the box's menu bar. If it's the wrong box, click on cancel and start again.

Creating a new workbook

What you will learn in this unit

By the end of this unit you will be able to:

- enter text and numbers
- edit spreadsheet data
- copy entries
- copy a block of cells
- erase data from cells
- move data to another location
- copy data to another location.

Data ranges

(d.) Spreadsheets work with 'Ranges' of data. A range is a rectangular block of cells that is referred to by the top left cell and bottom right cell in the range, for example the range (or block) B2–G11 shown highlighted in the screen shot below:

	A	B	C	D	E	F	G	H
1	Expenditure							
2	Month	Jan	Feb	Mar	Apr	May		
3	Rent	200	200	200	200	200		
4	Electricity	20	22	18	15	15		
5	Household	150	145	145	150	150		
6	Travel	45	45	40	40	40		
7	Gas	10	10	8	6	6		
8								
9								
10								
11								
12								
13								
14								

Entering data

(d.) Excel calls each spreadsheet a workbook. Each workbook is made up of up to 16 sheets. The **Sheets** tabs at the bottom of the screen are used to move from sheet to sheet, but we will only be working with one sheet at a time. New workbooks contain three sheets, but more can be added.

We're going to create a spreadsheet to record expenditure over several months. In spreadsheets, the values we place in the individual cells are referred to by the cell reference (A1, A5, G7, etc.). When we tell Excel to add two cells together, as in =A2+B2, Excel looks at whatever values are currently entered into those cells and adds them, so if we change the value in either of these cells Excel will automatically update the spreadsheet by recalculating it.

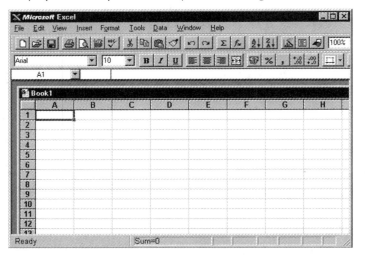

Your screen should have a double line border around cell A1, as in the screen shown above. This is the active cell, and anything you type will appear both in the cell itself, and in the formula bar just above your workbook.

If your screen has a different cell active, move the mouse pointer into the workbook area – it will change to a large white cross – and move the cross to cell A1 then single click (click once then release) the left mouse button.

Task 1: Entering data

1   Start Excel. Click **File, New** then double-click Workbook. A screen similar to the one below appears, with a blank workbook (called Book 1) ready for you to enter data.

	A	B	C	D	E
1	Expenditure				
2	Month	Jan	Feb	Mar	Apr
3	Rent	200	200	200	200
4	Electricity	20	22	18	15
5	Household	150	145	145	150
6	Travel	45	45	40	40
7	Gas	10	10	8	6

We are now going to enter the data in this spreadsheet.

2   Type Expenditure in cell A1 then press the *down arrow* key to move to cell A2. Don't worry if the word expenditure overlaps into cell B1 for now.

3   Type Month then press the *down arrow* key to move to cell A3.

4   Continue to type in the data shown above into your blank spreadsheet. Don't worry that the cells might be too narrow for some of the data, forcing it to overlap into the next cells.

5   Save your workbook by dropping down the File menu and clicking Save As. This dialog box appears.

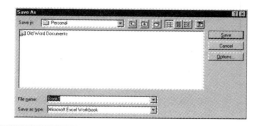

6   Save your work – type cash1 in the File name box near the bottom of the screen, then click **Save**. Excel automatically adds the extension .xls to your filename.

Making corrections and editing data

Sooner or later you are bound to make a mistake entering data. This is easily corrected.

Task 2: Editing data

1   Open cash1 if not already open.

2   Move the mouse pointer to cell C7 and click and release. The cell is highlighted and 10 appears in the formula bar.

3   Move the mouse pointer to the formula bar and click once to the right of 10.

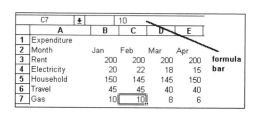

4   Use the *Backspace* key to delete 0, then type 5 and press *Enter*. Cell C7 now contains the value 15.

Task 3: Replacing cell data

1   Make cell C7 active by clicking on it.

2   Type 10 and press *Enter*. C7 will now contain the value 10.

Task 4: Deleting cell contents

1   Move to cell C7 and click to select.

2   Press the *Delete* key – the cell becomes blank.

3   Drop down the Edit menu and click Undo to reinstate the 10. Excel 97 allows 16 levels of undo.

Use the replace method when the data is completely different, and the edit method to correct minor errors such as spelling mistakes etc.

Copying and moving data

Copying data

Copying data leaves the original data intact and places a copy of it somewhere
else. For example, regular items of expenditure such as rent, insurance premiums,
travel costs, etc. are often the same from month to month, so rather than retype
the same data, it is more efficient to copy the data to the desired location.
Copying data is particularly appropriate when preparing cash flow forecasts.

Task 5: Copying data

1 Open the cash1 spreadsheet you created earlier if not already open.

2 Change cell B3 to 225.

3 Move the mouse pointer to cell B3, hold down the mouse button and drag to
   select cells B3 to F3, then release the mouse button. The value will be copied.

4 Save your modified spreadsheet.

Moving data

When you move data, you delete or cut it from its original location and place (or
paste) it somewhere else, for example, in the cash1 workbook, the data entered for
March may really be May's data.

Task 6: Moving data

1 Open cash1 if not already open.

2 Select cells D3 to D7 as shown in
   the screen.

	A	B	C	D	E	F
1	Expenditure					
2	Month	Jan	Feb	Mar	Apr	May
3	Rent	200	200	200	200	200
4	Electricity	20	22	18	15	15
5	Household	150	145	145	150	150
6	Travel	45	45	40	40	40
7	Gas	10	10	8	6	6

3 Click the **Cut** icon on the toolbar
   (the scissors symbol). Note that the
   bottom left of your screen displays:
   Select destination and press ENTER
   or choose paste.

the Cut icon

the Paste icon

4 Move to cell F3 and click.

5 Press *Enter*. The data will be moved from March to May.

This sequence of actions is known as 'cutting and pasting'.

Remember that if you make a mistake, you can undo your last action by dropping down the Edit menu and clicking Undo.

Practise with copy

Now select the data for May and copy it back to March so that both columns show the same data.

Entering numbers as text labels

Sometimes you may want Excel to treat a number as text. For example you may have a list of candidates numbered 1, 2, 3, 4, etc. To enter numbers as labels, precede each one by an apostrophe: '1997, '4, etc.

AutoComplete

If a label is already present on a worksheet, Excel's AutoComplete will automatically complete the label after you type the first few letters.

Using formulae and functions

What you will learn in this unit

By the end of this unit you will be able to:

■ generate new values using formulae

■ use functions

■ use absolute and relative cell addressing

■ use sum and average functions

■ use automatic and manual recalculation.

Entering formulae

Task 1: Entering a formula

1 Start Excel and create a spreadsheet with the data shown below: (You can use cash.xls).

	A	B	C	D	E	F	G	H
1	Expenditure							
2	Month	jan	Feb	Mar	Apr	May	Jun	Jul
3	Rent	200	200	200	200	200	200	200
4	Electricity	20	22	18	18	18	18	18
5	Household	150	145	145	145	145	145	145
6	Travel	45	45	40	40	40	40	40
7	Gas	10	10	8	8	8	8	8
8	Power							
9								

Cells B8, C8 etc. should contain a formula.

2 Move the pointer to cell B8.

3 Type =B4+B7.

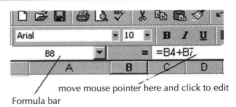

move mouse pointer here and click to edit
Formula bar

Formulae and functions always begin with an = sign. Cell B8 shows b4+b7? You forgot the equals sign before the formula. To correct this, click as shown below in the formula bar and type the = sign, then press the *Enter* key.

4   Move the cursor to cell C8 with the **arrow** key. Cell B8 should show 30.

5   Check the formula is correct in the formula bar (see Step 3).

     Look at the formula bar. It displays the contents of the current (active) cell. With formulae and functions, the formula bar shows the formula, while the cell shows the result of the formula, but you can make the worksheet display cell formulae instead of cell contents. This is useful to check the basis of your calculations. See Displaying and printing formulae below.

6   Look at cell B8; you will see the result of the formulae in cells B8, C8 etc., rather than the formulae themselves.

7   Now repeat the appropriate formula for cells C8, D8, E8.

8   Save your worksheet as **Cash2.xls**.

Mathematical operators in spreadsheet formulae

In computer work, we use + and – for add and subtract, but we use * for multiply and / for divide. Just as in maths, we sometimes have to use brackets around part of a formula, to change the order of precedence (the order in which the calculation is performed).

Percentages are usually represented by their decimal equivalent (the same as dividing the percentage by 100 – you move the decimal point two places to the left), so the current VAT rate, 17.5%, becomes .175.

More complicated formulae usually have their own functions, which are shortcuts to save having to enter long or complicated formulae, for example the SUM command.

Editing formulae

You can edit formulae just like any other cell entry.

1   Move the cursor to the formula bar with the mouse, clicking once.

2   Make the desired changes.

3   When you have finished editing the formulae, press the *Enter* key for the changes to take effect.

Displaying and printing formulae

You often want to see the formulae used rather than the results of the formulae. For example, college students' tutors will need a printout of their students' worksheets with the formulae to check their work.

Task 2: Displaying and printing formulae

1. Drop down the Tools menu and click on Options. This screen appears.

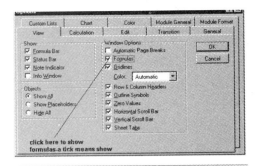

click here to show
formulas–a tick means show

2. Click the **View** tab, then click Formulas, and on **OK** to display cell formulae.

   You can switch Formulas off by clicking to remove the tick in the Formulas box.

3. To print the worksheet with formulae displayed, follow the above instructions to display formulae then drop down the File menu and click on Print Preview. If the layout is satisfactory, click on the **Print** button. Otherwise, see the section on printing and layout.

Using functions: the SUM function

The SUM function is used for adding up groups of cells. Functions are shortcuts for commonly used formulae. It has been estimated that around two thirds of all occasions when a spreadsheet function is used it is the SUM function, used to add up a range of cells. Because SUM is so common, Excel has a SUM function icon on the toolbar for you, as a handy shortcut.

Task 3: Using the SUM function

1. Open **cash2**, the spreadsheet you were working with in Task 1, if it's not already open.

2. Move the mouse pointer to cell G9.

3. Click the **SUM function** icon on the toolbar.

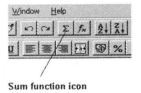

Sum function icon

   A flickering dashed line appears around the cells G3–G8. These are the cells to be added up.

4 Press *Enter* to see the total in cell G9.

The total should be 411. If not, you may have accidentally highlighted the wrong range. If you see the following box:

it' s because you accidentally included cell G9 in the range. Go back to cell G9 and click the **SUM** button again, then press *Enter*. Don't move the mouse after pressing the **SUM** button.

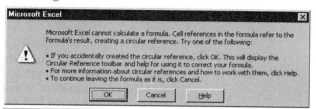

Copying formulae and functions

Task 4: Copying formulae

1 Re-open **cash2** if not already open.

2 Click on cell G9 (the cell containing the SUM function).

3 Drop down the Edit menu and click Copy. A message appears at the bottom left of the screen which tells you to select the destination and press *Enter*. Do this now, copying the formula to B9.

4 Click on cell G9, hold down the left mouse button and drag the mouse to cell B9, then release the mouse button and press *Enter*. Your spreadsheet should look like this.

Note: to switch between displaying values and formulae, click Tools, Options, Formulas.

Notice how the formulae in row 9 are automatically adjusted to take account of the fact that they refer to different columns. This facility is known as Relative Addressing (see the section on Absolute and Relative Addresses). Spreadsheets work with cell references rather than the actual numbers in the cells, so the spreadsheet 'knows' that when you copy the function from B9 to C9, etc., that it should update the column letter.

The average function

The second most commonly used function is the average function.

Task 5: Using the average function

1 Start a new spreadsheet workbook by dropping down the File menu and clicking New. Type in the following data:

	A	B	C	D	E	F	G
1		Jan	Feb	Mar	Apr	May	Jun
2	Rainf mm	100	75	80	86	54	45

Sheet1 / Sheet2 / Sheet3 / Sheet4 / Sheet5 / Sh

2 In cell H2 type the following formula: =average(b2.g2) and press *Enter*.

Cell H2 should contain 73.33 (there may be more decimal places – don't worry).

If you don't have the right answer, you may have chosen the wrong range or missed a bracket. If you get a message: #NAME?, you misspelled average. You have to type average in full, not just Avg.

Look at the formula bar. It should look like this:

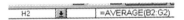

| H2 | ↓ | =AVERAGE(B2:G2) |

Note that when you enter formulae it doesn't matter whether you use capitals or lower case, or full stops instead of colons.

Automatic and manual recalculation

Normally, Excel will automatically recalculate the entire spreadsheet each time you change a value in a cell. However, with large spreadsheets this can slow down processing to an unacceptable level, so in such circumstances you can switch off automatic recalculation while you make changes.

Task 6: Switching off automatic recalculation:

1 Drop down the Tools menu and click Options. This screen is displayed.

2 Click on the **Calculation** tab, then click the **Manual** button.

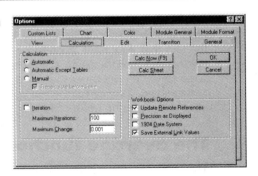

You can see from the above screen that there are several recalculation options available in Excel 97, but for now you only need to concern yourself with automatic and manual recalculation.

You can switch automatic recalculation back on in the same way. Note that when you start up Excel, it defaults to automatic recalculation.

Absolute and relative addresses

In our cash2 workbook when we wanted to total expenditure for each month, we copied the SUM function from cell B9 to successive columns, making use of the relative addressing facility.

If we had wanted the formula to remain exactly the same as that in B9, we would have had to use absolute addressing. Absolute addressing is used where we don't want the formula to be adjusted. For example a company would probably just store the current VAT rate in one cell, which they could use in a formula to give the retail price, as in the Task 7 below.

Excel Help has more information: type cell references.

Copying formulae using absolute addressing

As we said above, you need to be careful when copying formulae. If you want the formula to remain exactly the same regardless of its position on the spreadsheet, you should use absolute addressing rather than the default relative addressing. For example, a sales spreadsheet may contain the current VAT rate in one cell, with retail prices being obtained by multiplying the item's price by the current VAT rate and adding this value to the basic price. In this situation, you should use absolute addressing. It will also make life much easier to update prices if the VAT rate increases, since there will be only one cell to worry about rather than dozens or even hundreds of cells.

Task 7: Copying a formula using absolute addressing

1   Create the spreadsheet shown below and save as **VAT**.

	A	B	C
1		Net Price	Tot Price
2		5.99	=B2+(B2*A10)
3		6.49	
4		9.99	
5		7.69	
6		3.99	
7			
8			
9	VAT Rate		
10	0.175		
11			

Note that the total price is the net price plus VAT. The current VAT rate, 17.5%, is expressed as a decimal in cell A10. The formula in C2 says 'take the price in B2 and add to it the value of the price × VAT rate'.

2   Now copy the formula from C2 to C3. The following screen will appear:

C3		=B3+(B3*A11)	
	A	B	C	D
1		Net Price	Tot Price	
2		5.99	7.04	
3		6.49	6.49	
4		9.99		
5		7.69		
6		3.99		
7				
8				
9	VAT Rate			
10	0.175			

Note that the **Tot Price** in cell C3 has not been updated. Look at the formula bar and you will see the reason: relative addressing has changed the reference to cell A10 to A11, which is blank, so the formula is incorrect.

55

3 Click on cell C2 and edit the formula to =B2+(B2*A10) by inserting $ signs before each row and column reference for the VAT rate cell. The $ signs tell Excel to use absolute addresses.

4 Copy the formula to cells C3 to C6. The formula should show the correct amounts, as in the screen below:

C3	↓	=B3+(B3*A10)	
A	**B**	**C**	**D**
1	Net Price	Tot Price	
2	5.99	7.04	
3	6.49	7.63	
4	9.99	11.74	
5	7.69	9.04	
6	3.99	4.69	
7			
8			
9	VAT Rate		
10	0.175		

On your own

Think of some other situations where you should use absolute addressing.

Formatting spreadsheets

What you will learn in this unit

By the end of this unit you will be able to:

- left and right justify text
- change column width
- use integer and decimal formats
- format and justify character and numeric data
- insert rows and columns
- delete rows and columns
- change justification of data.

Changing column width

Task 1: Changing column width

1   Start Excel and either open an existing spreadsheet or use a blank new one.

2   Move the mouse pointer to the position shown below in the column header. When the black cross appears, hold down the left button and drag the mouse to the right to increase the column width by the required amount.

move mouse pointer to here until a thin black cross appears

	A	B
1	Expenditure	
2		

If you get a large white cross, it's because you moved the mouse down into the cell. Try again, keeping the mouse in the grey column header.

Task 2: Changing cell widths

1   Open the **Cash1** spreadsheet created earlier.

move mouse pointer to here until a black cross appears

	F	G
	May	Jun
	200	200

2   Move the mouse pointer to the position shown in the screen. When the black cross appears, hold down the left button and drag the mouse to the left to reduce the cell width.

3 Now practise changing cell widths for other columns.

Task 3: Changing width of all cells (columns) in a spreadsheet

Changing all cells is known as global formatting.

1 Open a spreadsheet (it can be a new one without data for this example).

2 Select the entire worksheet by clicking the **Select All** button at the top left corner of the worksheet. The worksheet changes to white on black.

If you make a mistake, you can remove the selection by pressing the **Home** key.

3 Drop down the Format menu, click Column, then click Width.

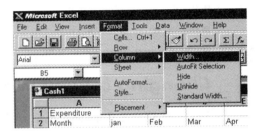

The Column Width box should appear.

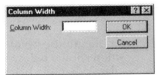

4 In the Column Width box type 30, then click **OK** . Your worksheet cells should all increase in width.

5 Click the **Undo** button to revert to the previous cell width.

Note: cell widths can be from 1 to 255, and indicates the number of characters that can be displayed using Excel's Standard font.

Inserting and deleting columns

Task 4: Insert a column

1 Move to cell B2 and click.

2 Click the Insert menu, then click Columns. A blank column will be inserted before (to the left of column) B.

You can click anywhere in a row or column to insert a blank row or column. Columns are always inserted before the highlighted column.

3   Click **Undo** to restore your worksheet.

Now practise inserting blank rows and columns in your spreadsheet workbook. Use **Undo** to restore the worksheet.

Task 5: Deleting column contents

Note that this operation leaves a blank column on your spreadsheet which you can re-use for other data. See below for how to remove the column completely.

1   Move the mouse pointer to the column G header and click to select column G.

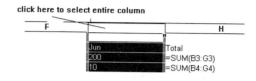

click here to select entire column

F		H
	Jun	Total
	200	=SUM(B3:G3)
	10	=SUM(B4:G4)

2   Press *Delete* – the column contents will be deleted.

If you accidentally delete some data, you may be able to recover it if you realise straight away and click Edit to drop down the edit menu, then choose Undo. Practise this now with column C.

Task 6: Removing columns, rows, and cells completely

1   Select the desired column, row, or cells as before.

2   Drop down the Edit menu and click Delete.

If you are deleting a group of cells, a further dialog box asks whether you wish to move cells down, to the right, etc.

Inserting and deleting rows

Task 7: Inserting a row

1   When you insert a row, it is inserted above the current row, so if you want to insert a new row above row 6 (between rows 5 and 6), place the cursor on a cell in row 6 and click.

2   Click on the Insert menu to drop it down.

3   Click Rows to insert a blank row between rows 5 and 6.

Inserting a row inserts the row above the selected row.

Task 8: Deleting row contents

Note that this operation leaves a blank row on your spreadsheet which you can re-use for other data. See previous section for how to remove the row completely.

1 Move the mouse pointer to the row
2 header, as shown, and click to
select the row.

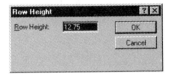

click here to select entire row

2 Press *Delete* to remove the contents of the row.

Changing row height

This is very similar to changing cell width.

Task 9: Changing row height

1 Select the desired range of cells (or click the select all button)

2 Click Format menu, Rows, Height.
This dialog box appears.

3 Insert the row height in points and
click **OK**.

A point is one-sixth of an inch, and
there are 6 points to a standard line, so
a row height of 12 points is equivalent
to two lines.

Inserting cells

As well as inserting complete rows and columns, you can also insert just a few
cells, but this is a bit more tricky than inserting complete rows or columns.

Task 10: Inserting cells

1 Open an existing or new spreadsheet.

2 Select cells C4 to D5 by moving the
mouse pointer to cell C4, holding
down the left mouse button and
dragging the mouse pointer to cell
D5, then releasing the left button.
The cells should be highlighted.

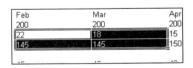

Be careful that you don't copy cell C4
to the other cells by mistake.

3 Drop down the Insert menu and click Cells. This dialog box is displayed.

You will see that you can choose whether to move the cells down, to the right, etc.

4 Click **OK** to shift the cells down.

Use the Help if you are not sure what each option does.

Data types and data formatting

In spreadsheets, there are two main kinds of data: text, and numeric data (which includes formulas and functions). The different types of data are formatted differently by most spreadsheets, and actions such as adding, subtracting, summing, etc., cannot be performed on text data, only on numeric data.

In Excel, text data is left aligned by default, and numeric data is right aligned, as in the example below:

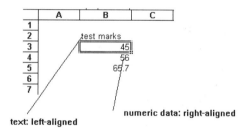

However, once you have completed your data entry you may want to change data justification, for example to line up numbers under a column heading.

Alignment of data

Task 11: Changing data justification

1 Start Excel, open a new workbook and enter the test marks data in the screen above.

2 Save your spreadsheet as test1.

3 Select the cell B2.

4 Click on Format Cells to display the Format box.

5   Click the **Alignment** tab to display this dialog box.

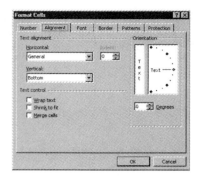

6   Click the **Horizontal, Right** button to line up the test marks heading with the marks.

You should note that in spreadsheet work numbers are always right aligned and text left aligned, so text and numbers don't line up. This lets you instantly see if you accidentally enter an o instead of a 0 (zero), and lets you tell at a glance whether your data is numeric or text. You should always align headings to numbers and never align numbers to headings.

Formatting cells

Cell formatting is concerned with the display of numeric data, for example how many decimal places to display, etc.

Task 12: Formatting cells

1   Create a new workbook with the following data and formulae (the heading has been aligned with the marks; you don't need to do this).

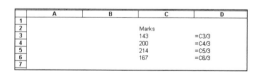

2   Select column D by clicking on the column heading.

3   Drop down the Format menu and click on Cells. This screen will be displayed.

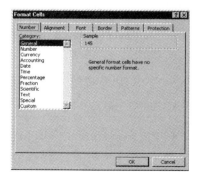

4   Click on Number.

5   Use the **down arrow** in the Decimal Places box to set to 0. Click **OK** .

6   Now repeat the formatting, but this time format the cells to two decimal places.

7   Again, repeat the formatting operation, but this time to four decimal places (0.0000).

8   Finally, format the same cells to eight decimal places. This screen will appear.

	A	B	C	
1				
2			Marks	#######
3			143	#######
4			200	#######
5			214	#######
6			167	#######

The ##### symbols indicate that the cell is too narrow to display the data in the chosen format. However, if you increase the cell width sufficiently, the data will be displayed to eight decimal places.

9   Increase the width of column D until the data is displayed.

10 Now change the formatting back to two decimal places, and reduce the column width to a suitable width.

Printing and layout

What you will learn in this unit

By the end of this unit you will be able to:

- preview your workbook before printing
- produce printed copy of a spreadsheet
- print in landscape mode (sideways)
- change paper size
- fit your workbook to one page
- change margins
- use headers and footers
- set print area
- print only part of your workbook.

Previewing your work

Task 1: Previewing a printout

1   Open the **cash1** workbook (any other spreadsheet would do).

2   Click on the File menu and click on Print Preview. A screen similar to this should appear.

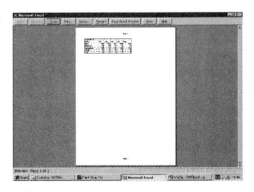

You won't be able to read your text, as preview is just for checking the layout. If you click on the **Zoom** button, it magnifies the worksheet. Clicking on zoom a second time returns you to the miniaturised view.

3 Press *PgDn* to move through your worksheet if it is more than one page long.

4 Before printing, make sure your printer is switched on, is loaded with the appropriate paper, and is on-line.

The majority of problems that people have with computers are to do with printers, so don't be surprised if you need help.

5 If you are happy with the layout of your document, click on the Print button to obtain a printout. You should see a message on screen telling you that your file is being printed, and on which printer.

6 Click the **Close** button to close Print Preview.

Printing your worksheet in landscape mode (sideways)

Worksheets are often wider than they are long, so it is often best to print them sideways on, known as Landscape mode.

Task 2: Printing landscape

1 To select landscape mode, click on the File menu, Page Setup; this screen will appear.

2 Click on the **Landscape** button.

Changing paper size

The Setup dialog box also allows you to choose different paper sizes. The most common size is A4, but you will also often come across US letter, which is 11" by 8.5". You can change paper size by clicking on the arrow to the right of the Paper Size box and selecting the appropriate size.

Fitting your worksheet to one page

You can often reduce the size of your worksheet to one page.

■ Click on the Fit To: box and type: 1 page wide by 1 page tall.

■ If you need to make changes to your workbook before printing, click the **Close** button to return to your workbook.

You should always preview your workbooks before printing.

Adjusting margins

Again, this is done from the Setup dialog box. Click the **Margins** tab and enter appropriate sizes, remembering to note whether the sizes are given in inches or centimetres.

Headers & Footers: titling your worksheet

From Page Setup click on the **Header/Footer** tab to display the headers and footers box (shown below). Use the header box for the title of your worksheet.

It's also a good idea to include a footer with the name of your worksheet so that you can find it again on your disk.

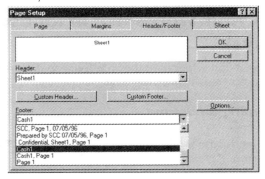

■ Click the **down arrow** in the footer box.

■ Scroll through the list and click on the workbook name (e.g. cash2.xls).

■ Click on **OK**. The workbook name will appear in a footer when you print the worksheet.

Printing selected cells

Task 3: Printing selected cells

1 Open the **cash1** workbook created earlier (any other workbook will do).

2 Click on the **row 4** button (or any other row containing data) to highlight the entire row.

3 Click on File, Print Area, Set Print Area. The preview screen should only display the selected cells (row 4).

4 If the preview is satisfactory, click the **Print** button to print out only row 4.

5 Click on File, Print Area, Clear Print Area to reset the Print area.

Creating charts and graphs in Excel

What you will learn in this unit

By the end of this unit you will be able to:

■ select relevant data

■ produce pie charts

■ produce bar charts

■ change chart type

■ add and change chart headings, labels and text

■ delete, copy and move charts

■ adjust the size of charts

■ export charts to other applications.

12.1 Entering data and creating a Pie chart

Task 1: Creating a Pie chart

1 Start Excel

2 Enter the data shown into the workbook:

	A	B	C	D	E
1	Expenditure				
2	Month	Jan	Feb	Mar	Apr
3	Rent	200	200	200	200
4	Electricity	20	22	18	15
5	Household	150	145	145	150
6	Travel	45	45	40	40
7	Gas	10	10	8	6

3 Save your spreadsheet as **cash3**.

4 Select cells A1 to B7.

	A	B	C	D	E
1	Expenditure				
2	Month	Jan	Feb	Mar	Apr
3	Rent	200	200	200	200
4	Electricity	20	22	18	15
5	Household	150	145	145	150
6	Travel	45	45	40	40
7	Gas	10	10	8	6
8					

5 Click on the **ChartWizard** tool on the toolbar. This will start the Office Assistant, to guide you through creating a chart.

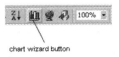

chart wizard button

6 Follow the instructions in each step of the Wizard. The Assistant explains each step.

7 At step 4, click **As object in** sheet 1, then click **Finish** .

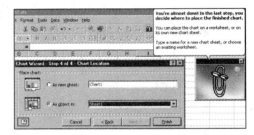

Your chart should be displayed with the spreadsheet, with segment names, % and titles, and should look similar to the screen below:

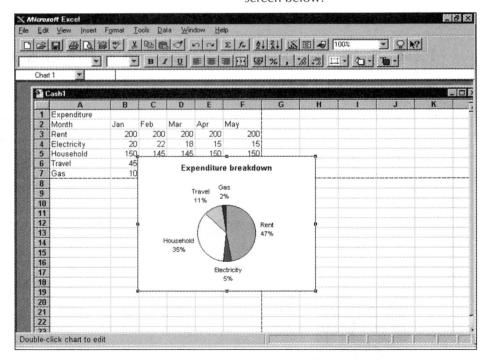

8 To customize your chart, click **Get help with customizing a chart** in the Office Assistant box.

Creating charts and graphs in Excel

9 Your chart is now finished. Save as **cash3** – your chart is saved with the spreadsheet. This type of chart is known as an embedded chart and is saved with its worksheet.

Note: You can also save charts separately.

Creating bar charts and other types of chart or graph

Excel calls vertical bar charts column charts, and horizontal ones bar charts.

■ The procedure for creating a bar chart or column chart is exactly the same as that for a pie chart, except that at Step 1 of the ChartWizard you should select Column or Bar, as required.

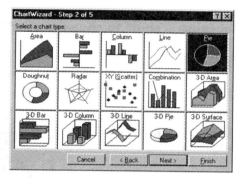

■ Similarly, at Step 1 you can select any of the other types of chart displayed.

Note that not all types of data are suitable for all chart types, although you can usually produce bar charts for most types of data.

Changing the type of chart

Quite often you will not be happy with the type of chart that you have selected. In Excel it is very easy to change the chart to another type.

Task 2: Changing the chart type

1 Open the **cash3** workbook if not already open

2 Display the Chart toolbar by dropping down the View menu and clicking Toolbars, then select Chart, **OK** .

3   Click on the **down arrow** on the
    Chart Type button to drop down
    the chart type icons.

chart type button

4   Change the chart type by clicking on a different chart type. You can experi-
    ment with as many chart types as you like.

Creating charts when data range is not continuous

Task 3: Creating a chart to show expenditure for February

1   Open **cash3** if it is not already open.

2   Select cells A2 to A7.

3   Hold down the *Ctrl* key and, while
    holding it down, select cells C2 to
    C7. Your screen should be similar to
    this one.

	A	B	C	D	E
1	Expenditure				
2	Month	Jan	Feb	Mar	Apr
3	Rent	200	200	200	200
4	Electricity	20	22	18	15
5	Household	150	145	145	150
6	Travel	45	45	40	40
7	Gas	10	10	8	6
8					

You can include other ranges (blocks)
of cells by keeping the *Ctrl* key pressed
while selecting cells.

You can move the ChartWizard box out
of the way by dragging it if you want to
see your worksheet.

4   Click on the **ChartWizard** and
    create a column chart. Your screen
    should look similar to this one.

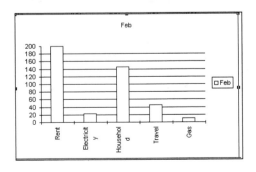

If your chart doesn't appear to show any data, you probably included some other cells, probably A1 and/or C1. If so, delete your chart and re-select the correct range.

5 Now display the chart toolbar and change the chart into a pie chart.

Sizing graphs and charts

Task 4: Sizing a chart

1 Open the **cash3** workbook created earlier. A screen similar to this one should appear:

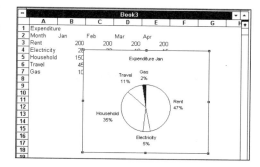

(d.)

Note the small black markers at each corner and mid-way along each side of the chart. These indicate that the chart is selected, and are called selection squares.

2 Click on the mid-point marker on the right-hand side, hold down the left mouse button and drag the mouse to the right about one inch (3cm), then release the mouse. The width of the chart will have increased.

3 Now practise the same operation on the mid-point marker of each of the other sides of the chart.

4 Now try the above, but this time on one of the four corner markers.

Note that when you use these techniques, the whole chart changes in size, but it retains its original proportions.

5 Now use the same technique to reduce the size of the chart.

Deleting charts

Task 5: Deleting a chart

1 Make sure the chart is selected (the small black markers are visible). If not, move the mouse pointer into the chart area and click and release the left mouse button once.

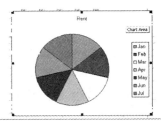

2 Press Delete to delete the chart.

If the chart is still present, you may have double clicked – see the instructions above.

Moving charts and graphs

You may want to move an embedded chart so that you can see the worksheet data, or you may want to move your chart so that it covers the data up.

■ Make the chart active if it is not already as described earlier.

■ Move the mouse pointer into the chart area.

■ Hold down the left mouse button and drag the chart to the desired position.

Practise this now on your own.

Chart headings and labels

The parts of the Excel screen are shown below:

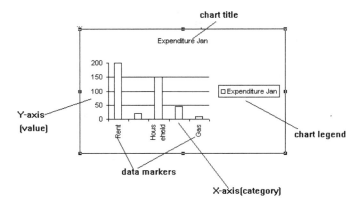

When you create charts using the Wizard, as in Task 1, you are given the option of adding titles, legends, etc., depending on which type of chart you are using. However, sometimes you will not be happy with the results and will want to change or format the headings and labels.

One approach is to simply delete the existing chart and start again, using the ChartWizard to make appropriate choices at each step. if you are unsure what to choose, you can click Help for advice.

Note that if you increase the size of the chart this may solve problems like the one shown below, where the labels electricity and household don't fit very well.

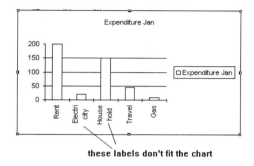

these labels don't fit the chart

However, if you increase the height of the chart, you can make them fit better.

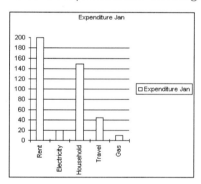

Editing chart items

Task 6: Editing chart items

1   Open the **cash3** worksheet if not already open.

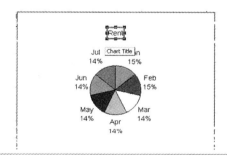

2   Click the chart title. Selection markers (small black squares) will appear around the selected item.

3   You can move or size the title in the same way that you can move or size a chart. Click the title box and drag it up by about one inch (3cm), then release the mouse.

4 You can format the title by selecting it, then double clicking to display a screen similar to this one.

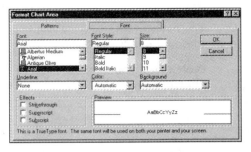

Note that the exact options available will depend on the item selected.

5 Click on the **Font** tab to display the above screen, then change the size of the font to 10 point and click **OK** .

Other chart items can similarly be selected then formatted using similar procedures.

Adding text to a chart

Task 7: Adding text to a chart

1 Re-open the **cash3** if not already open.

2 Drop-down the View Menu, click Toolbars, Drawing.

3 Click the **Text Box** icon on the Drawing toolbar

4 Draw a text box inside the chart area in the position shown below:

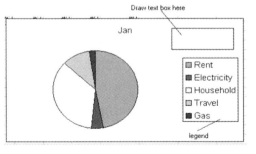

5 Click inside the text box. A flashing text cursor will appear. Now type Household Expenditure.

You can use the same procedure for any other text that you want to appear in charts.

Adding a legend to a chart

Task 8: Adding a legend to a chart

1   Open **cash3** and its associated pie chart.

2   Display the Chart toolbar, if not already present, by dropping down the View menu and clicking Toolbars, Chart.

3   Click inside the pie chart, then click once on the **add** or **delete legend** button on the Chart toolbar. The legend will be added if not already present, and removed if it is currently present.

add/delete legend button

The chart with legend displayed (months of the year) will look similar to this one.

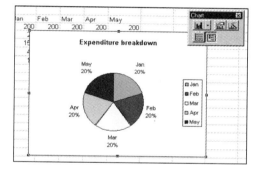

You can also add or delete a legend from the Chart, Chart options menu.

Adding gridlines to a chart

Task 9: Adding gridlines to a chart

1   Click Chart, Chart options to display this box.

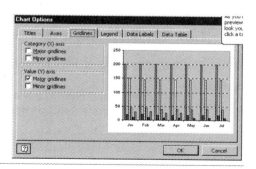

2 Click the **Gridlines tab** and tick the gridlines boxes required.

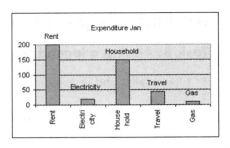

Adding data labels to a chart

Task 10: Adding data labels to a chart

1 Open **cash3** or another Worksheet chart.

2 Drop-down the Chart menu and click Chart options.

3 Click on the **Data Labels** tab.

4 Click on Show label and percent. Your screen should look similar to this.

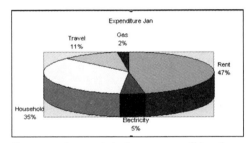

If some of your labels are cut off by the chart border, you can click on them and drag them to a new position in the chart.

  For help on adding labels, titles etc., use the Excel Help.

Changing chart scales

Task 11: Changing a chart's scale

1 Open the **cash3** workbook and its associated chart if not already open.

2 Change the chart type to a bar chart using the Chart toolbar **Chart Type** button. If the chart is not present, recreate a bar chart to show expenditure for January.

3   Display the chart and double-click on the Y-axis (the value axis) on the left-hand side of the chart. The Format Axis box should appear.

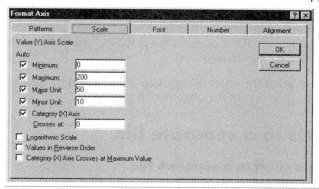

4   Click once on the **Scale** tab to display the screen above.

5   Change the minimum value to 10 and the maximum value to 600, then click **OK** . The scale on your chart will change to reflect the new values.

6   Now change the scale back to minimum 0, maximum 200.

 Often, you can leave Excel to automatically set the values, but sometimes you are instructed what values to show in your scale.

Exporting graphs and charts to other applications

Task 12: Exporting a chart to Word

1   Open Excel and the **cash3** worksheet created earlier.

2   Click once on the chart to select it. Change the chart to a pie chart. (If you have no chart, use the ChartWizard to create a pie chart for January's expenditure).

3   Drop down the Edit menu and click Copy.

4   Start Word by clicking on the **Start** button, **Programs**, **Microsoft Word**.

5 Drop down the File menu and select New,   .

6 Click on Edit, Paste. The Excel chart will appear in your Word document.

 You can size the chart within Word in the same way that you can in Excel, by clicking inside the chart to make it active, then grabbing one of the marker squares and dragging the chart to size.

You can centre or left align the chart in your Word document by clicking to select the chart, then clicking on one of the alignment buttons.

Saving charts to a separate file

Task 13: Saving a chart to a separate file

1 Open the **cash3** workbook created earlier.

2 Select the pie chart for January.

3 Click on the **Copy to Clipboard** icon on the toolbar.

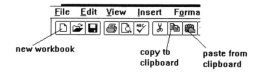

4 Click on the **New Worksheet** icon on the toolbar.

5 Click on the **Paste** icon on the toolbar. Your chart will appear in a new blank worksheet.

6 Save your worksheet with a new name.

 You can also use the Chart Menu, Location option to save a chart as a new sheet or an object in another sheet.

Section 3
Access 97

Introduction to databases and Access 97

What you will learn in this unit

By the end of this unit you will be able to:

■ start up Access

■ understand basic database concepts

■ use Access Help.

Introduction

The idea of a database is very simple; it's the electronic equivalent of a filing cabinet or a box of index cards (or any other kind of filing system).

Access is a database management system (DBMS).

Computer databases use a few jargon terms:

Database	the electronic equivalent of a filing cabinet or card index box.
Table	equivalent to a drawer in a filing cabinet. A database may have a single table, but in business it will often have several tables, such as 'Customers', 'Suppliers', 'Orders', 'Stock', etc.
Record	equivalent to an individual card in a card index, for example, a customer address record card, or a stock record card.
Field	equivalent to each data item in a record: each line on the record card below; each category of information in a record.

These correspond to data on an index card as shown in the diagram below:

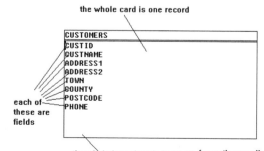

Starting Access

Task 1: Starting Access

1 Switch on your computer and click on the **Start** button at the bottom left of the screen.

All instructions to click mean press and release the left mouse button once only. Right click means press and release the right mouse button once only.

2 Move the mouse pointer to Programs, then across to Microsoft Access, then click on Microsoft Access as shown in the screen. You will notice that Access is added to the Taskbar at the bottom of the screen:

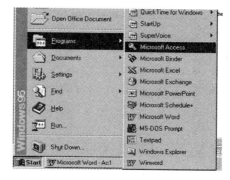

If nothing seems to happen, try repeating the above instruction. Make sure that the highlighting is on Programs, and then on Microsoft Access.

For now, we are just going to see how to use Help in Access.

3 Click **Cancel** .

If this is the first time you have used Access, the Office Assistant will start up.

 You can also start Access from the Office toolbar, by clicking on the **Key** icon at the right-hand end of the toolbar in the screen below:

Exiting from Access

Click on the File menu, then click Exit. Any work will automatically be saved for you.

Using Help

To use Help:

■ Click on the Help menu, then click on Contents and Index to display the following screen:

■ Click on the topic you want, then click **Open** .

Using Help to find a particular topic

There is a topic on using Help from the Help Topics screen shown above. It is suggested that you look at this now. Point to Getting Help and click Ways to Get Assistance, Display.

Task 2: Finding a Help topic

1 Click on the Help menu, then click on Microsoft Access Help to display the Office Assistant.

2 Type in your question then click **Search** .

It is recommended that you click Getting Started with Access and choose the appropriate option.

Printing out Help topics

You can get a printout of any Help topic by clicking the **Options** button and clicking Print Topic. See the screen below:

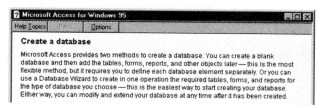

On your own

Use Help to revise the topics that we have covered so far. If there are any that you want to print out, do so. You may like to build up your own file of Help topic printouts for future reference.

Creating a new database

What you will learn in this unit

By the end of this unit you will be able to:

■ create record structure

■ enter data

■ save data

■ exit from Access with data secure

■ modify an existing database structure.

Creating a database structure

Task 1: Create a new database

1 Start Access (see previous unit). This screen should appear.

2 Click on **Create a New Database Using Database Wizard** button, then click **OK**.

This screen should appear.

3   Click **OK** to select Blank Database.

4   Type the Filename Employee in the
    file name box in this screen.

Filenames can be up to 255 characters,
with spaces and full stops as well as
letters and numbers. However, if you
want to use your database with Version
2 of Access, or if you want to use it on
other computers using Windows 3.11
or 3.1, filenames must be limited to a
maximum of 8 characters, with no
spaces or punctuation marks. You
should try to use meaningful abbrevia-
tions wherever possible, e.g. UKSales5
could be the data for UK sales in 1995.

You now need to choose whether you are going to save your database on floppy
disk (Drive A:) or the hard disk or network, and in which folder (directory).

5   To change to a different folder or
    drive, in the Save In box click on the
    down arrow to show the avail-
    able folders and drives.

    This screen will appear.

6   To change to a different drive, in the Save In box click on the **down arrow**
    to show the available drives (31/2 floppy A, Disk 1 C etc).

7   To save your work on a floppy disk, insert a formatted disk with sufficient
    room for your data in the floppy drive and double click the 31/2 Drive (A:)
    icon.

8   Choose C: and the My Documents folder to save your Employee database in.

9   When you've finished choosing
    drive, folder and filename, click the
    Create button. A window similar to
    this will appear.

10 Click **New**. This box appears.

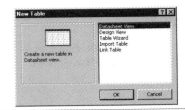

You are now going to create a database table with the following fields and enter some records into the database:

surname	DOB	phone	married	wage	service

11 Click Design View then click **OK**. This screen appears.

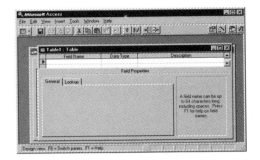

12 In the first row of the Field Name box type Surname then press *tab* once. The screen should look like this.

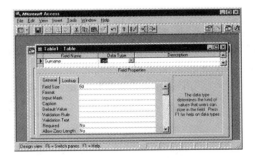

Notice that the data type is automatically set for text.

13 Move the mouse pointer down to the Field Size box, delete 50 and type 10.

14 Move the mouse pointer to the Required box and click. A **down arrow** appears. Click on this and click **Yes**. This stops users from entering a record without filling in the surname.

15 Move to the next field, and call it **DOB** for date of birth.

16 Press *tab* to move to the Data Type box, click once in the box to display the **down arrow** , then click once on the **arrow** . Click once on Date/Time.

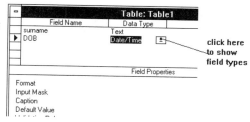

click here
to show
field types

Notice that we don't have to specify the length of date fields. Access does it automatically.

17 Move to the third field name, call it **phone** with data type text and field size 12.

Using text data type allows us to use brackets and hyphens.

18 The next field is going to be called **married**, field type Yes/No. Create it.

Yes/no fields like this are known as Boolean fields.

19 Now create a field **wage** of type currency, and a field **service** of type number, Field Size single. When you are in the field size box press the *F1* function key to display the Help box about field size properties. It is recommended that you print out this Help topic for future reference.

We have now finished creating our database table structure.

20 Click on File menu, Save to display this box.

21 Type the name Staff in the Table Name box and click **OK** . This box will appear.

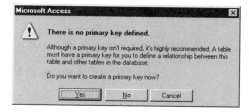

22 Click the **No** button. The table structure will then be saved.

23 Click the File menu, Close.

24 To exit from Access, drop down the File menu and click Exit.

It is recommended that you use the Assistant to search for information on Primary Keys.

25 Open the **Employee** database

26 Open the **Staff** table by selecting Staff and clicking the **Open** button.

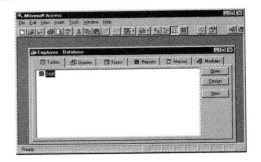

27 A data entry screen like this will appear

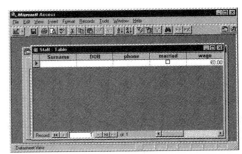

Enter the following records into the table:

surname	DOB	Phone	married	wage	service
Smith	08/09/46	01344-235786	Yes	£230.00	19
Jones	05/02/73	01344-584765	No	£190.00	3
Sutton	24/05/67	01370-234896	Yes	£300.00	7
Bold	15/09/62	013709-98566	Yes	£250.00	8
Higgins	20/06/59	013444-55824	No	£380.00	20

28 Now enter some more records into the table. Create some fictitious records then click on the File menu, Close to save your work and close the table and database. There should be at least 10 records in your table.

Some important database concepts

Field names

These should be meaningful, shorthand expressions without spaces or punctuation, such as SNAME (surname), FNAME (first name), DOB (date of birth), ADDRESS1 (first line of address), TOWN, PCODE, PHONE, etc. You can't have two fields with the same name. Keep addresses in separate parts for town, county, etc. as this makes searching by town, county, etc. much easier.

Field types

- Text for text and whole numbers that aren't going to be used in calculations (e.g. age, 'phone number)

- Date/Time for dates and time

- Number for decimals and numbers that are going to be used in calculations, e.g. sales figures

- Currency for money

- Yes/No for true/false logical values, e.g. a "married" field could be logical.

Field length

This has to be fixed, so you need to plan your database structure beforehand (although you can alter the length later).

Required fields

This box is for when you want to force the user to enter data in a field.

Primary keys

These are used to sort the records to allow fast access. Access encourages you to choose one field as the primary key field, and then sorts the records on this field. However, only one record with the same value is allowed in the primary key field, for example if you choose surname for the primary key, you can only have one Smith, Jones etc. For this reason, you should always choose a numeric or a counter field for the primary key: don't use surname as the primary key field.

Modifying database structure

You would only need to do this if you found that you had made a mistake such as setting a primary key field on a name field etc., or if you needed to add a field or change the properties of a field.

Task 2: Modifying the employee database structure

1   Open the **Employee** database, **Staff Table**.

2   Click on the View menu, click
    Design View to display this screen.

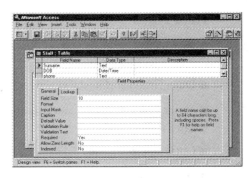

Access has two main views: Data Sheet
View for working with data, and Design
View, for creating and changing database structures, reports, forms and
queries.

This is the same screen as the one we
saw when creating our database table
structure.

3   Click on the Indexed field box to
    display a drop-down menu; the box
    to the right explains the options.
    Read this box now.

Note that no primary index is currently
set, and is indicated by the absence of
the key symbol against any of the fields
(see the screen below for an example
from a different table, with a primary
key set on the Customer ID field).

primary
index key
indicator

4   Double-click the **Close** button in the top left of your screen, beside staff:
    Table.

Primary keys

Note that no primary key is set on Staff. This section is for information only.

If you find that a table you are using won't let you enter data and displays an error message about duplicate entries not being allowed in the primary key field, you have probably inadvertently set the primary key. Primary keys are a useful feature, but should only be used on a numeric field (such as an account number), and not on surname fields (just think of all those Patels and Joneses).

Task 3: Setting a primary key

1   Choose View, Design view.

2   Click the **Indexes** button on the toolbar.

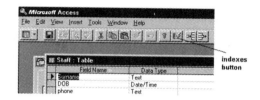

3   Select the row with the primary key indicator and press *Delete*.

4   Drop down the File menu and click on Close to save the changes.

You can also set or disable the Primary Key setting from the Edit menu, by toggling Primary Key on or off:

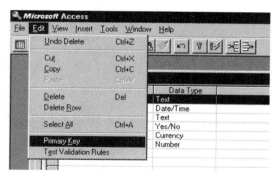

Opening and moving around an existing database

What you will learn in this unit

By the end of this unit you will be able to:

■ navigate around an Access database table

■ save records, tables and databases.

(!) Note that this unit uses the employee database that we created in unit 14. Make sure this is available for use. Alternatively, you can follow the tasks using the Northwind sample database, supplied with Access.

Opening a database

Task 1: Opening the employee database

1 Start Access. A screen similar to this one will appear.

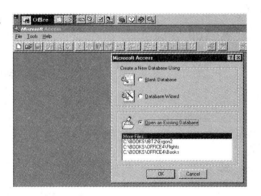

2 Click Open an Existing Database, OK . We are going to open the **Employee** database. Move the mouse pointer to Employee in the File Name box and double-click to open the employee database. This screen should appear.

Note that Access uses the term Database to refer to all the files associated with an application. Access uses the term Table to refer to each of the different data files such as customers, suppliers, orders, etc. If you have used other database packages such as dbase, the Access equivalent of a dbase database (.dbf) file is a Table. All the files and tables etc. related to a particular database are stored under the database filename.

Opening and displaying a database table

The Employee database is now open and the last screen in Task 1 is displayed, with a list of the tables available, just the Staff table that we created earlier.

Task 2: Open and display the database table

1 Move the mouse pointer to the Staff Table and click **Open** . You should then see a screen similar to this one.

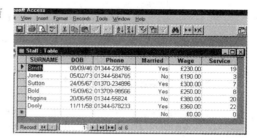

As many records as will fit on the screen are displayed. If there are too many to fit the screen, you will need to scroll down to the next screen by pressing the *PgDn* key. Each row is a record (for example, Smith, Jones), and each column is a field (for example, Phone, Wage, etc.).

Opening databases created in previous versions of Access

If you try to open a database from a previous version of Access, the following screen is displayed:

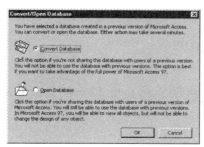

Read the advice, then choose an option or click **Cancel** . See Help for more advice on working with databases from earlier versions.

Moving and resizing Access windows

In Access, you often need more than one window open at a time. You can move and resize each window, and overlap several windows, as in the screen below:

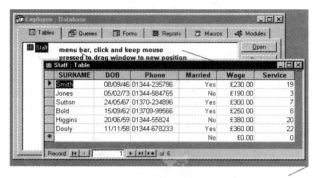

to re-size window, move mouse pointer to
corner until 45 degree arrow appears, then
drag to re-size

Task 3: Resizing a window

1   Use the information in the above screen to practise resizing the Staff Table window by dragging it at its bottom right corner.

2   Click on the menu bar of the Employee database window to make it active and bring it to the front. Notice how the Staff window is now hidden from view.

3   Click on any part of the Staff   If you can't see any part of the Staff
window to return the screen to its   window, drop down the Window menu
previous appearance, as above.   in Access and click on Staff, Table.

Moving around the table

You can move around the table using the mouse or keyboard in the normal Windows ways, but you can also use the **VCR** buttons at the bottom of the screen to move to the first record in a table, the last record, the previous record or the next record (see the next screen).

■ *Tab* moves to the next field.

■ *Home* moves to the beginning of a record (beginning of row).

■ *End* moves to the end of a record.

■ The mouse can be used to click on and select any field you want to edit.

■ The Scroll bars can be used with the mouse to move around the table.

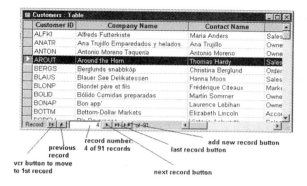

record number: 4 of 91 records

previous record

vcr button to move to 1st record

add new record button

last record button

next record button

On your own

Practise moving around the table now. Move to the first record using the **VCR** button, then the **last record** button, and scroll through using the vertical (right-hand) scroll bar. Use End to move to the last field in the current record, then Home to move to the first field in the current record.

Closing and saving databases and tables

Access saves your work as soon as you move from one record to another, but it is important to exit properly from Access to make sure that your data is secure.

Closing tables

Choose Close from the File menu. The table will automatically be saved to disk. Always close tables when you are not working on them to prevent the possibility of accidental data loss.

Closing databases

Choose Close from the File menu. You can double-click the Close box in the window instead.

Exiting from Access

Drop down the File menu and click on Exit.

Note that all changes you make in databases and tables are automatically saved for you. The action of moving the cursor to a new record tells Access to save changes to that record.

Working with files on floppy disks

You will find that Access runs much more slowly if you work from floppy disks. You may also find that large databases are too big to fit on floppy disks. For these reasons, it is not recommended that you work from a floppy disk. Instead, you should copy your database from the floppy disk to your computer's hard disk.

Task 4: Opening a database on a floppy disk

1   Start Access.

2   Click the **Open Database** button on the toolbar.

3   Insert a floppy disk with your Access database on it into the disk drive.

4   Click on the **down arrow** in the Look in box and scroll to display 3½ Floppy (A). All databases will be displayed.

5   Click on the database you want to open, then click the **Open** button.

Your File Name doesn't appear in the File name box? This is most likely because you gave it an extension other than .mdb or it's a different kind of file, for example an Excel or Word file. By default Access only shows Access database files. To show other types of file, click on the **Files of Type box arrow** and click on All Files, then click **OK**.

Task 5: Saving a database to floppy disk

1   If you are working with a database on a floppy disk, then it will automatically be saved back to floppy disk.

2   To save a database on a different drive, including a floppy, choose the Save As/Export command on the File menu. This screen will be displayed.

You should check the size of the database before copying to a floppy, as Access databases can become too large to fit a floppy disk.

On your own

Practise opening databases on drive A: and saving databases to floppy disk.

You can't save your database? Check that it's not too big to fit.

Adding new data and editing a database table

What you will learnin this unit

By the end of this unit you will be able to:

■ enter data and new records

■ edit data

■ delete a record.

Adding new records

1   Open the **Employee** database, **Staff** table.

2   Move to the last record, then use the _down arrow_ key to move down to the blank new record row at the end of the table .

3   Now type in the following new fictitious record in the blank row.
    Dooly   11/11/58   01344-678233   Yes   £360.00   22

    Note that if the record is already there, just make up your own fictitious record.

Possible problems when adding or editing data in tables

You shouldn't have any problems with Task 1, but may encounter problems with other tables, in the future.

A box similar to the one below appears on screen?

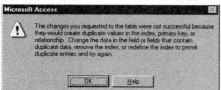

This box will appear if you enter a new record with the same customer ID as an existing record. This is because there is a primary key set on customer ID in this table.

  Primary keys are used by Access to index the data and display it in order. Only one record is allowed with a particular primary key field value (such as WHITC in the customer table) so that you can't accidentally enter the same record twice. However, this means that you should always choose as a primary key a field where each value will occur once only. For this reason, you should not use fields such as surname, but should instead use unique numbers such as national insurance or bank account number. Use Help to go through this, as it's a confusing topic.

To continue entering data, change the value in the primary key field. If you want to enter a duplicate value, you should read the Access Help topic on primary keys and then delete the primary key field. See Chapter 14 for information on this.

A box similar to the one below appears on screen.

This is because when the table was created the 'Staff' field was set so that a value had to be entered. This is a useful way to validate data input in databases. You should click on **OK** then enter the relevant data in the company name field.

Changing (editing) existing data

Place the cursor in the field you want to edit, using either the mouse or the cursor keys. If the data is highlighted, typing will automatically delete the existing data in the field. To remove the highlighting, move the mouse pointer into the table and click the left button once.

Deleting records

To delete a record

1 Place the cursor in the box to the left of the record (row) to be deleted and click once. An arrow will appear next to the record, and the whole row (record) will be highlighted, as shown below:

SURNAME	DOB	Phone	Married	Wage	Service
Bold	15/09/62	013709-98566	Yes	£250.00	8
Higgins	20/06/59	01344-55824	No	£380.00	20
Jones	05/02/73	01344-584765	No	£190.00	3
Smith	08/09/46	01344-235786	Yes	£230.00	19
Sutton	24/05/67	01370-234896	Yes	£300.00	7
Dooly	11/11/58	01344-678233	No	£0.00	0
*			No	£0.00	0

2 Press *Delete* or select Edit, Delete Record from the menus.

3 The box below asks you to confirm the deletion, or cancel it. Click **Yes** to delete.

Inserting new records in a table

To insert a new record

1   Click on the Records menu and click Data Entry. The following screen appears:

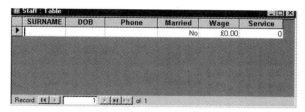

2   To add a new record to the table, type in the new details. You add the new record at the end of the table. Access automatically inserts the records in sequence for you, so there is no facility to enter records directly into the middle of the table. You can add as many record as you like.

3   Click File, Close to save the changes and close the table.

 When using primary key indexes, Access will automatically insert records in their proper sequence. If you don't have a primary key and wish to Sort your records you will need to use the **Sort** button.

Moving and copying records

Moving a record deletes it from its present location and places it in the new location. Copying a record leaves the original record in place.

You can't make an exact copy of a record in the same table if you have set a primary key, since primary keys only allow one record with the same primary key field. You should not usually set a name field as the primary key field – just think how many Joneses, Smiths or Patels there are.

You can copy and move either complete records or individual data using the Windows Clipboard: choose the Edit menu and Cut (for moves), or Copy (for copies) options from the menu. Move the cursor to the new location, then choose Edit, Paste to complete the copy or move.

 You can use the clipboard to copy data from Access to other applications, such as Word or Excel, as well as to many other applications. However, not all applications will accept the formatting of your data. You can also use the clipboard to copy data from other applications to Access.

Displaying and searching for data

What you will learn from this unit

By the end of this unit you will be able to:

■ sort records alphabetically and numerically

■ select records by a single criterion

■ select records by multiple criteria

■ present specified fields from selected records

■ print a sorted list of records

■ print the results of a single condition search

■ print out one selected record only

■ print selected fields only.

Introduction

Datasheet view (the normal screen that we see when using tables and databases) displays all the data in a database table, but often we only want to see certain fields, or only records that meet certain criteria, such as 'all employees earning more than £15,000 who are female', etc. To display such a selection of data, Access uses Queries. A query is based on a table or tables, and searches for data that match the specified criteria.

This unit uses a database that you need to create before working through the examples.

Create a database called **dblabel**, with a table called **Labels** and containing the data shown below:

Code	Widthmm	Heightmm	Across	No persheet	Price	Sheets	Remarks
8361	80	24	4	32	£21.99	100	mail label
8362	80	36	4	24	£22.99	100	mail label
8363	80	48	4	16	£13.99	50	mail label
8364	90	36	3	24	£23.99	100	small parcel
8365	90	48	3	16	£12.99	50	large mail
8366	100	24	3	16	£12.99	50	large mail
8367	100	36	3	12	£12.99	50	small parcel
8368	100	48	3	8	£12.99	50	parcel
8369	200	48	1	4	£11.99	50	parcel

Creating a query

Task 1: Creating a query

1   Open the **dblabel** database but don't open any tables.

2   Click the **Query** tab, then New. This screen should appear.

3   Click Design View, **OK** . This screen should appear.

4   Click Labels, then click **Add** to base the query on the labels table.

5   Click on **Close** in the Add Table box. The fields of the labels table are displayed.

6   Click on CODE, hold the mouse button down and drag the field into the field box like in this screen.

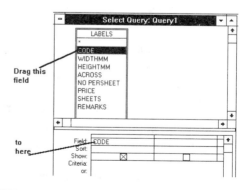

7   Repeat for HEIGHT and PRICE fields, dragging them into the second and third columns as shown in Step 9.

8 When you have finished, click File, Close and click **Yes** to Save changes to query.

9 Name your query **CODE** in the Save As box and click **OK** .

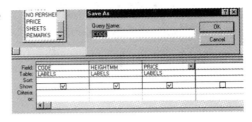

10 Your query is now saved. Look at the query list box and scroll down until you see the CODE query.

11 Click on CODE to select it, then click the **Open** button. This screen should appear.

12 Your query should display only the contents of the CODE, HEIGHTMM and PRICE fields, for all records in the table (there are nine records).

13 Now add two more fields to your query, Across and Remarks, and open it to see the results.

Selecting all fields equal to a given value

We use this to search for, for example, all employees under 40, or paid more than £15,000 per annum or all labels priced £12.99.

Task 2: Searching for all labels priced £12.99

1 Open the **dblabel** database if it is not already open.

2 Click the **Query** tab, then click New.

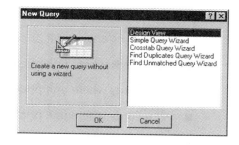

3 Click Design View, then click **OK** . This screen should be displayed.

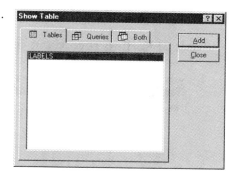

4 Click on **Add** .

5 Drag CODE to the Field1 box.

6 Repeat for the PRICE field.

7 Click on Criteria under PRICE and type =12.99.

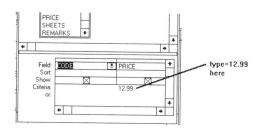

8 Click File, Close and name the query **Price**.

9 Open the query. You should see a list of all records where unit price = 12.99

10 Now create separate queries for each of the following search conditions:

■ All records where unit price is less than (<) 12.99

■ All records where unit price is greater than (>) 12.99

■ All records where unit price is not equal to (<>) 12.99

■ All records where unit price is less than or equal to (<=) 12.99

■ All records where unit price is greater than or equal to (>=) 12.99.

Sorting records

Task 3: Sorting records in ascending order

1 Select the PRICE query and click the **Design** button. A screen similar to this should appear.

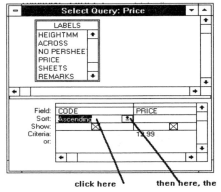

2 To sort in ascending order, click in the Sort field then click on the **arrow** , then click Ascending.

3 Close the query, save changes, then select and open it. The records are displayed in ascending alphabetical order.

4 Now create a new query, using the LABELS table, to display CODE, PRICE and HEIGHTMM sorted into ascending price order.

5 Open your query; it should look like this.

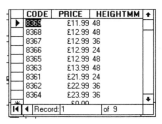

Task 4: Selecting records by date: finding all employees born since 1965

1 Open the **Employees** database created earlier in Unit 14.

2 Go to Query, New.

3 Add the Staff table.

4 Select the fields SURNAME and DOB

5 Under criteria in birth date type >=01/01/65. Your query should look similar to this.

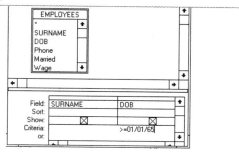

6 Close the query and save as **EmpAge**

7 Open the query. Your screen should be like this one.

SURNAME	DOB
Jones	05/02/73
Sutton	24/05/67

Record: 1   of 2

Selecting records by more than one criteria

Task 5: Displaying all three across labels 36mm or higher

1 Open the **dblabel** database.

2 Go to Query, New.

3 Use the **Labels** table

4 Drag the **CODE** field to field 1.

5 Drag the **ACROSS** field and set criteria =3

6 Drag the **HEIGHTMM** field and set criteria >=36.

7 Close the query and save as **HEIGHT**.

8 Open the query to check the results. Your screen should be similar to this one.

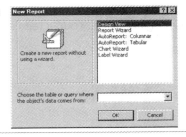

9 Now practise using more than one criteria in queries on your own. You just drag the fields you require and fill in the criteria box.

Reports: printing selected data

A report is a printout of a selection of data from a table or query, so you need to select the appropriate table or query first. Generally, unless you want the whole table printed out, you use a query as the basis for a report. You then save the query and can re-use it each time you want the same selection of data, even if the data in the table has changed. See the section on creating a query earlier in the unit and the Access Help for more details.

Task 6: Creating a report

1 Open the **dblabel** database and click Reports.

2 Click **New**. A screen similar to this one is displayed.

3 Highlight the Report Wizard and click **OK**. This screen is displayed.

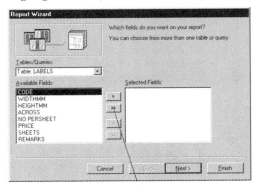

4 Click the **Select all fields** button.

5 Click **Finish** to let Access design your report. The report will appear similar to this screen.

Wizards are automated procedures for doing commonly performed tasks, and make life easy for beginners.

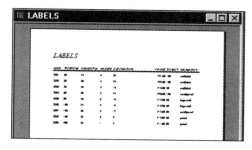

6 Move the mouse pointer into the body of the report. A magnifying glass symbol will appear. Click on this to alternately increase and decrease the magnification of the report.

Chapter 19 deals in more depth with producing reports in Access.

 Your report may be too large to fit on your screen. You can use the horizontal scroll bar to view more of your report.

Printing your work

What you will learn in this unit

By the end of this unit you will be able to:

■ Print data from an Access database.

Note that printing out selections of records that meet search criteria is dealt with in Unit 17: Displaying and Searching for data.

Previewing your work

Task 1: Using print preview

1 Open the **dblabel** database, **labels** table.

2 Click on the File menu and click on Print Preview. A screen similar to this one should appear.

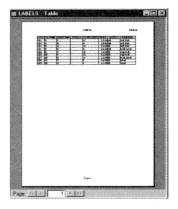

Don't worry if you can't read your text, as Preview is just for checking the layout.

3 Move the mouse pointer into the page; a tiny magnifying glass icon appears. If you click on this, it magnifies the selected text.

4 Press *PgDn* to move through your document if it is more than one page long.

Task 2: Printing

1 Before printing, make sure your printer is switched on, is loaded with the appropriate paper, and is on-line.

2 Use Print Preview to make sure your work looks OK.

The majority of problems that people have with computers are to do with printers, so don't be surprised if you need help. If you have recently upgraded to Windows 95 and are having problems printing from all your applications, you may need a new printer driver from the supplier of your printer.

3 If you are happy with the layout of your document, click on the **Print** icon to obtain a printout. You should see a message on screen telling you that your file is being printed, and on which printer.

Print layout and page orientation

Task 3: Changing layout and orientation

1 If you need to make changes before printing, click the File menu, Page Setup option to display this screen.

2 Move the mouse pointer to the left margin box, highlight the 1.000in by clicking and dragging, then type 1.5. You don't need to add 'in' or the extra 000s.

3 Click the **Page** tab.

4   Click the **Landscape** button to print your table out sideways.

You should always preview your documents before printing.

If your printer flashes a message such as "Load letter" this is because you are either out of paper, or the wrong paper size has been chosen in the Page Set-up box. To change paper size, move to the Paper Size box and click on the **down arrow** to drop down the list of paper sizes, then double-click on the correct size. You may need to check which size to use. In the USA, the standard size is US letter 8½ by 11", in Europe it is A4 210mm by 297mm.

If you get a "Paper jam" message or other message there is probably paper jammed in your printer. Consult your printer manual.

Designing reports in Access

What you will learn in this unit

By the end of this unit you will be able to:

- create reports in table format

- save data, reports, data subsets

- print reports.

Introduction

Reports are used to print out data. They are similar to forms and queries, but offer more control for printing out data. A report is based on a table or query, but allows you to select and group data. Mail labels are a special kind of report. Access 97 provides Wizards to automate report design, but you can go back and change elements of the design after your report is finished.

Note that to complete this section, you need the **WKSTN** table, which you will have to create yourself, using the information given at the end of this unit. Create the **Equipment** database, **WKSTN** table, with all fields text, 10 characters long.

Designing tabular reports

A tabular report is used to print out all or selected fields/records in a table rather like a spreadsheet, where each record is a separate row in the table. An example is shown in this screen.

WKSTN				
17-Dec-95				
REF NO	**SFTWARE**	**LIGHTS**	**USER**	**DEPT**
CA503	Yes	Yes	Yes	Admin
CA504	No	No	Yes	Sales
CA505	Yes	No	Yes	MIS
CA506	No	No	No	Sales
CB203	Yes	Yes	Yes	Mktng
CB204	No	No	No	Admin

Task 1: Designing a tabular report

1   Open the **Equipment** database   If this isn't available, you can create it
    WKSTN table.   using the data at the end of this unit.

2   Click the **Reports** tab, then click
    New. This screen will be displayed.

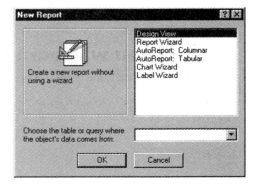

3   Click Auto Report: Tabular.

4   Click the **down arrow** in the   If **WKSTN** isn't displayed it may be
    Choose the table or query where   because you haven't created it yet.
    the object's data comes from box   Create it from the information at the
    and select WKSTN.   end of this unit.

5   Click OK to display this screen.

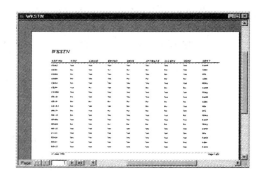

    Access has automatically created a
    simple report in tabular (spreadsheet)
    format.

6   Save your report as **Tabular Report**.

Creating Reports using the Report Wizard

Task 2: Creating a report with Report Wizard

1 Click the **Reports** tab, then click
   New. This screen will be displayed.

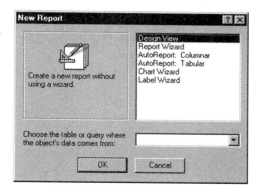

2 Choose the **WKSTN** table from the
   Choose table... box as before.

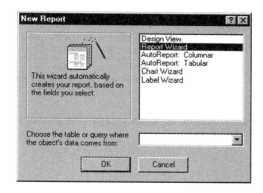

3 Click Report Wizard, **OK** to display this screen.

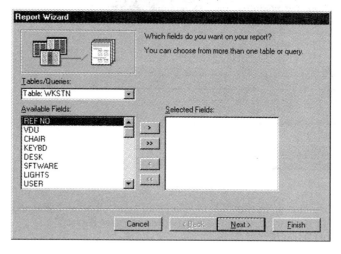

4   Select REF NO in the Available fields box, then click the `>` button to place REF NO on the report as the first field.

5   Repeat for SFTWARE, LIGHTS, USER and DEPT fields, then click `Finish`. Access designs a report similar to this one (it may take a minute or two).

WKSTN1		
REF NO	*SFTWARE*	*LIGHTS*
CAS03	Yes	Yes
CAS04	No	No
CAS05	Yes	No
CAS06	No	No
CB203	Yes	Yes
CB204	No	No
CC2058	Yes	Yes
CD120	Yes	Yes

Note that if you had wanted to sort the records, you could have chosen `Next` instead of `Finish` at the last stage, which would have allowed a sorting option.

6   Drop down the File menu and click Save As. Name your report **Workstation 2** and save it in the current database, then click `OK` to save it.

7   You can preview your report and print it by dropping down the File menu and choosing Print Preview.

Task 3: Changing the report

1   Display the Database window and click the `Report` tab.

2   Highlight **Workstation 2** (the report you just designed).

3   Click on the `Design` button to display this screen:

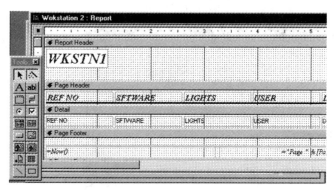

4   Place the mouse cursor in the report header and change WKSTN to Workstations.

You can type whatever you like for headers in your report.

5   Click on **File, Save** to save changes to your report.

Designing reports to group data

If you want your report to put all records for a particular department together, or to produce subtotals for different departments, you can use the groups/totals Report Wizard.

Task 4: Grouping data in a report

1   Open the **WKSTN** database (if this isn't available, any other Access 97 database will do).

2   Click the **Report** tab, then click **New**.

3   Click Report Wizard.

4   Drop down the list of tables and queries in the Select a Table/Query box and click on WKSTN.

5   Click **OK**.

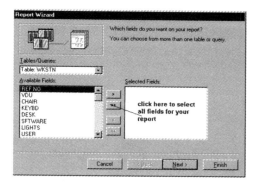

6   Click the **double arrow** button to select all fields for your report, then click **Next**.

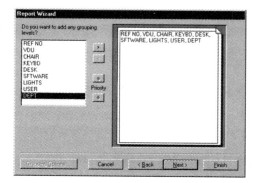

7   Scroll down to DEPT in the Do you want to add any grouping levels box, select it and click the > button to group your records by department, then click **Next**. A screen similar to this one will appear.

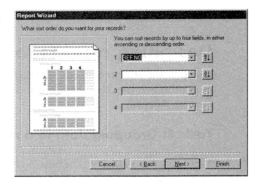

8   In the You can sort records by up to four fields... box drop down the arrow and select REFNO then click **Next**.

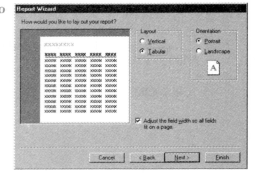

9   Click **Next** to select the default report layout.

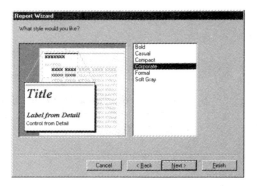

Note that by default, all field widths will be adjusted to fit one page.

10 Accept the default settings by clicking **Next** .

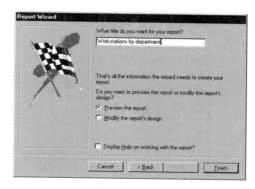

11 In the box, type in the title Workstations by department, then click **Finish** . Access will now finish designing your report, and will display a screen similar to this one.

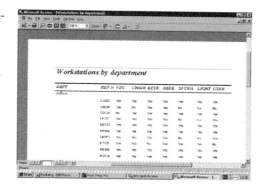

Note that the workstations are grouped together in their departments.

12 Your report is now complete. To obtain a printout, drop down the File menu and click Print.

Publishing databases on the World Wide Web

Access 97 allows you to use database data to create Web pages. You are advised to use the Assistant for more information.

1 Click File, Save As HTML. The Publish to the Web Wizard starts, as shown below:

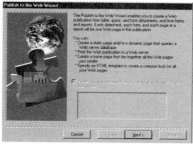

2 Click **Next** and follow instructions on each screen to publish your data on the web.

WKSTN table

The following table contains the data from the above database table, and may be used to create the table.

REF NO	VDU	CHAIR	KEYBD	DESK	SFTWARE	LIGHTS	USER	DEPT
CA503	Yes	Yes	Yes	Yes	Yes	Yes	Yes	Admin
CA504	No	Yes	No	No	No	No	Yes	Sales
CA505	No	Yes	Yes	No	Yes	No	Yes	MIS
CA506	No	Yes	Yes	No	No	No	No	Sales
CB203	No	Yes	Yes	Yes	Yes	Yes	Yes	Mktng
CB204	Yes	No	Yes	Yes	No	No	No	Admin
CC2056	Yes	Yes	Yes	Yes	Yes	Yes	Yes	Mktng
CD120	No	Yes	Yes	Yes	Yes	Yes	Yes	Admin
CD134	No	No	No	No	No	No	No	Sales
CD1342	No	Yes	Yes	No	No	No	Yes	MIS
MN134	No	Yes	No	No	No	No	Yes	MIS
MN123	No	Yes	Yes	Yes	Yes	Yes	No	Mktng
MP080	Yes	Yes	Yes	Yes	Yes	Yes	Yes	Admin
MP065	No	Yes	No	No	No	No	No	Mktng
ME123	Yes	Yes	Yes	Yes	Yes	Yes	Yes	Admin
CY123	Yes	Yes	Yes	Yes	Yes	Yes	Yes	MIS
RE456	Yes	Yes	Yes	Yes	Yes	Yes	Yes	Admin
RE134	Yes	Yes	Yes	Yes	Yes	Yes	Yes	Sales
RQ123	Yes	Yes	Yes	Yes	Yes	Yes	Yes	Admin
YO212	Yes	Yes	Yes	Yes	Yes	Yes	No	Sales
PO212	Yes	Yes	No	No	No	No	Yes	Sales
PT2211	Yes	Yes	Yes	No	No	No	Yes	MIS
PT121	Yes	Yes	No	Yes	Yes	Yes	No	Admin
LP232	Yes	Yes	Yes	Yes	No	No	Yes	Admin
SA212	Yes	Yes	Yes	Yes	No	Yes	Yes	Sales
SD1213	Yes	Yes	Yes	No	No	No	Yes	Mktng
SA423	Yes	Yes	Yes	Yes	Yes	Yes	Yes	MIS
SA237	No	Yes	No	No	No	No	Yes	MIS
OK872	Yes	Yes	Yes	Yes	No	No	Yes	Admin
LK234	Yes	Yes	Yes	Yes	Yes	Yes	Yes	Sales

Make all fields Text, 10 characters long.

Section 4
PowerPoint 97

Starting PowerPoint 97

What you will learn in this unit

By the end of this unit you will have covered:

■ presentations, slides, templates

■ starting PowerPoint

■ the PowerPoint opening screen

■ using Help.

Introduction

 PowerPoint is a presentation graphics program, and is used to produce overhead projector (OHP) slides or on-screen presentations.

The central part of a PowerPoint presentation is the slide, which corresponds to one OHP slide or one screen of a presentation. PowerPoint allows you to add your own text and graphics to a ready-made background template, making it easy for anyone to create an attractive presentation.

Slides can be accompanied by Speaker Notes, which are designed to be used by the presenter. Slides can also contain graphic images, either from the clip art supplied, or from another source such as a company logo.

Slides can also contain graphs and charts, organisation charts, or multimedia clips such as short (a few seconds) sound, animation or video clips.

The best way for new users to use PowerPoint is to use the existing templates and the Wizards, since they are based on accepted graphic design principles. You should only work from scratch when you are confident that you have a good understanding of graphic design. For most users, the supplied templates will prove adequate.

Starting PowerPoint

Task 1: Starting PowerPoint

1   Click the **Start** button, Programs,
    Microsoft PowerPoint, as shown in
    this screen.

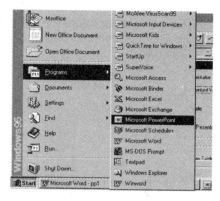

The opening screen, shown below, allows you to open an existing presentation or
create a new presentation. The AutoContent Wizard is the best way for new users
to create new presentations.

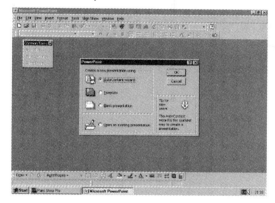

Using Help

Task 2: Using Help

1   Click on **Cancel** in the Create New Presentation screen.

2   Click on the Help menu to drop it
    down, then click Contents and
    Index to display this screen.

3   Click on the topic you are interested in from the list, then click **Open** .

4   If you can't see the topic you want, drop-down the Help menu and click Microsoft PowerPoint Help.

5   Type you request into the Office Assistant screen and click the **Search** button.

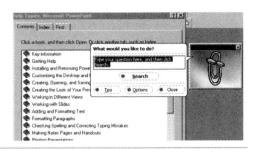

6   You can get a printout of any Help topic by selecting the topic, then clicking the **Print** button in the Options menu.

Some of the kinds of Help available in PowerPoint are shown below:

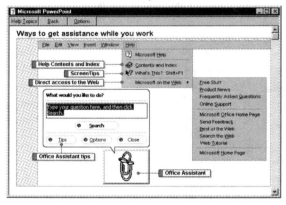

On your own

Use PowerPoint's Help Contents to get an overview of creating, opening and saving presentations.

Creating a new presentation

What you will learn in this unit

By the end of this unit you will be able to:

■ use the AutoContent wizard

■ create a new presentation

■ choose a template

■ choose type of output

■ create a new slide

■ choose the layout for a slide

■ give slides a title

■ add text to slides

■ spell-check your presentation

■ save your presentation.

Using the Wizards

Task 1: Creating a presentation using a Wizard

1　Start PowerPoint.

2　Drop down the File menu and click New.

3　Click the **Presentations** tab to display this screen.

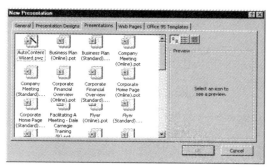

Note the various templates available for some common types of presentation. You can click on a template to see a preview of how it will appear.

4   Click on the **AutoContent Wizard**
    icon and click **OK**. This screen
    appears; with the Office Assistant if
    you need help.

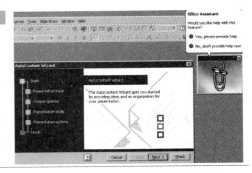

5   Click the **Next** button. The next
    screen asks you what type of presen-
    tation you want to create, with a
    brief summary to the right of the
    box.

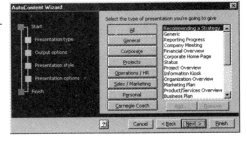

6   Choose one of the presentation
    types shown. If none of these is
    appropriate for your report, choose
    the General option from the box,
    then click Generic and the **Next**
    button.

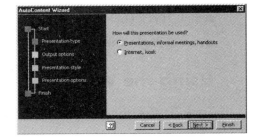

If this screen isn't displayed, you probably clicked Other instead of General.
Go back and try again.

7   Choose how the presentation will be
    used, then click **Next**. You can
    just accept the default settings by
    clicking **Next**.

8   Choose the on-screen presentation type of output using the screen at the bottom of the previous page, then click **Next** .

Before choosing your output, you should think about what equipment will be available for your presentation, and how you will cope if something breaks down. It is often a good idea to print a set of overheads, in either colour (preferably) or black and white, so that if all else fails you will only need an overhead projector to give your presentation.

9   Enter the information requested, then click **Next** .

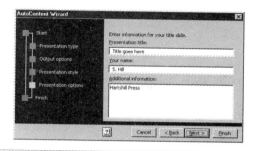

10 Click the **Finish** button to complete your presentation. You should see a screen similar to this one (assuming you typed in the information).

Note that your presentation already includes nine slides, and that this is slide 1 of 9.

Your screen is in outline view, and tells you what kind of information to place on each slide. You may find it useful to print out this screen to help you fill in your blank slides.

11 Drop down the **View** menu and click **Slide** .

12 Place the cursor at the start of the "Title goes here" and type your title.

13 Drop down the Insert menu and click New Slide.

You can also move to a new slide by clicking on the **New Slide** button on the toolbar.

14 From the New Slide box above, choose a slide Layout.

The default layout has a header and a single bullet list. Other options include two-column bullets, bullets and charts, charts only, organisational chart, bullet and graphic etc.

15 Choose the single bullet list and click **OK** .

A PowerPoint presentation is made up of one or more slides. Slides can contain text that you type in, but they can also contain graphs and charts, drawings, pictures (e.g. your company logo) and even sound and video clips. PowerPoint can also produce handouts and speaker's notes to go with your presentation. The slides can be run as an on-screen presentation, where it is shown on a computer, or it can be used to produce overhead projector or 35mm slides.

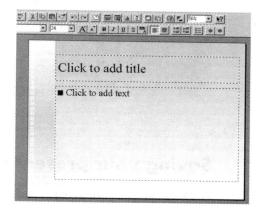

16 Click in the Title box to give your slide a title. Type: Starting PowerPoint.

17 Click in the main body part of the slide to type in text. Type in the steps for using the AutoContent Wizard that you have learned in this unit, but using your own words.

18 Click the **New Slide** button to move to the next slide, then repeat the above operations.

19 Create some more slides where you explain in more detail each step in using the AutoContent Wizard.

Spell-checking

Task 2: Spell-checking

1 Drop down the Tools menu and click on Spelling.

Note that PowerPoint automatically checks spelling as you work. Any word underlined with a red wavy line may be mis-spelled. Click on the underlined word with the right mouse button to see corrections.

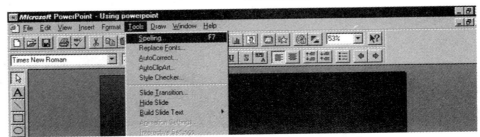

You can also click the ABC spell check button.

Saving your presentation

Task 3: Saving your presentation.

1 Drop down the File menu and click Save. This screen will be displayed.

2 Type Using powerpoint in the File name box.

3 Click Save to save your presentation.

4 Exit PowerPoint by dropping down the File menu and clicking Exit.

Viewing and printing a presentation

What you will learn in this unit

By the end of this unit you will be able to:

- open an existing presentation

- move through the slides in a presentation

- delete a slide

- change the order of slides

- use Outline and Notes views

- print slides, notes and outlines.

Opening a presentation

Task 1: Opening an existing presentation

1 Start PowerPoint.

2 Drop down the File menu and click Open. A screen similar to this one will be displayed.

You can look in different folders (directories) by clicking on the down arrow to the right of the Look in box and clicking Disk 1 vol 1 (C:), as shown in the screen.

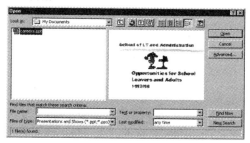

3 Find the folder with the **Using PowerPoint** presentation that you created in the last unit.

If you didn't create this presentation, you can either go back and create it now, or open a different presentation and try to follow the instructions as best you can. It only takes a few minutes to create the presentation.

4 Click on the Using PowerPoint file, then click **Open** . Your screen should look similar to this one.

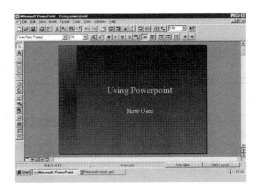

Moving through your slides

Your presentation should have 10 slides, and you should be on slide 1 of 10.

Task 2: Moving through the slides

1 Click once on the **Next Slide** button – the double down arrow on the lower-right of the vertical scroll bar – to move to slide 2.

2 Click once on the **Previous Slide** button – the double up arrow on the lower-right of the vertical scroll bar – to move back to slide 1.

The button is obscured by the Next Slide label in the screen shot below? You can also use *PgDn* to move to the next slide, and *PgUp* to move to the previous slide.

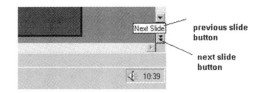

previous slide button

next slide button

3 To move to the last slide in a presentation press the *Ctrl* and *End* keys together.

4 To move to the first slide in a presentation press the *Ctrl* and *Home* keys together.

5 To move to a particular slide in a presentation click on the grey button in the vertical scroll bar and drag it by holding down the left mouse button until the slide number you want is displayed.

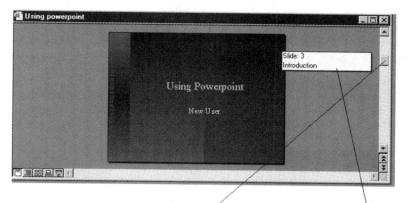

click on this button to display the slide number label. While holding down the left mouse button, drag the scroll bar button until the slide number you want is displayed

Another way to move straight to a particular slide is to go to Slide Sorter view from the View menu, then double-click on the slide you want to go to.

Inserting and deleting slides

Deleting a slide

To delete a slide drop down the Edit menu and click Delete slide.

Inserting a new slide into the middle of a presentation

To insert a slide:

■ Change to Slide Sorter View from the View menu.

■ Click on the slide before the one you want to insert. Your new slide will be inserted after this slide.

■ Drop down the Insert menu and click on New Slide.

■ Choose the screen layout. Create your new slide.

Adding a new slide at the end of a presentation

To add a slide at the end click on the **New slide** button on the toolbar (or use the Insert menu), then choose your slide layout etc.

 Note that you insert the new slide at the end of the presentation, and then you place it in the desired position in Slide Sorter View.

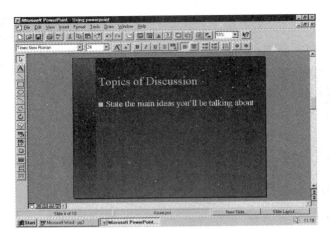

Changing the order of your slides

Task 3: Changing slide order

1   Drop down the View menu and click Slide Sorter to display your slides. Your screen should look similar to this one.

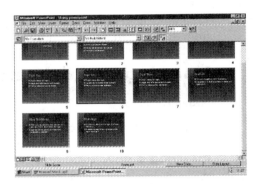

2   Use the mouse to click on the slide you want to move.

3   While holding down the left mouse button, drag the slide to the new position and drop it into place. A vertical line appears to the left of the new slide position.

When you drop a slide in place, the remaining slides are moved up. If you drop the slide into the wrong place, you can use the **Undo** button to undo the move.

Using different slide views

The following ways of viewing your presentation are possible. They are selected from the View menu.

View	Description
Slide view	The default view is used for creating and editing individual slides.
Slide Sorter view	Shows thumbnails (reduced-size images) of all your slides, and is used to change their order or to insert a new slide into the middle of a presentation.
Outline view	Displays just the text structure of the slides.
Notes page view	Shows slide with any speaker's notes.

On your own

Practise using the different views to look at your presentation (you haven't created any speaker's notes, so won't be able to use that view yet).

Views in PowerPoint

An example of Outline View is shown below:

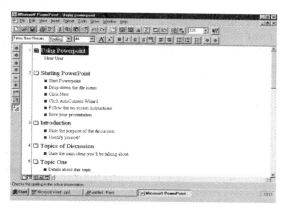

An example of Notes View is shown below (note that there are no notes attached with this slide, so the box is empty).

Printing your presentation

By default, printing a presentation will print out the slides full size. However, there are options to print out the slides (two, three or six slides reduced to fit on each page), handouts, notes pages or outline view.

If you are printing out OHP transparencies, you need to make sure that your printer is loaded with suitable transparencies.

 Note that there are special types of transparencies that must be used with inkjet and laser printers, and that they are not interchangeable. Using the wrong type, especially in a laser printer, can cause serious damage to the printer.

Even if you are going to give your presentation on screen, it is still a good idea to printout a copy for your own use. To be on the safe side, you may like to create a set of acetates (OHP transparencies) just in case there is a problem with the on-screen version or the equipment.

Task 4: Printing slides

1 To print the slides, using the system defaults, click the **Print** button on the toolbar.

click here to print slides

2 To print more than one copy of your slides, or to print handouts, notes, etc. or to change other options, such as printing to fit the page, drop down the File menu and click Print to display this box.

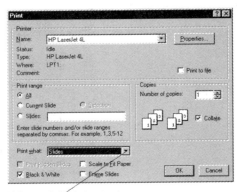

click here to print handouts, notes etc.

3 Choose what to print, whether to scale to fit, which slides to print, etc., from the options in the print box. Then click **OK** to print your options.

 It is often a good idea to print out a copy of your slides using the six slides per page option, to give you an overview of your slides.

Editing and adding images to presentations

What you will learn in this unit

By the end of this unit you will be able to:

- add slides to a presentation

- add pictures and charts to slides

- size and position pictures and charts

- add sound and video: multimedia presentations

- format slides.

Adding slides to a presentation

Task 1: Adding a slide

1. Start PowerPoint and open the **Using PowerPoint** presentation that you used in the last unit.

   If this isn't available, you can open any other presentation.

 2. Click the **New slide** button on the toolbar (or use the Insert menu)

   This button allows you to create a new slide at the end of your presentation. To create a new slide and insert it part way through a presentation see Unit 22.

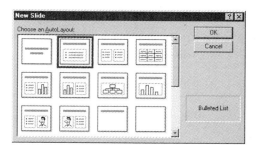

3. From the New Slide box, choose a slide layout.

4   Choose the single bullet list and click **OK**.

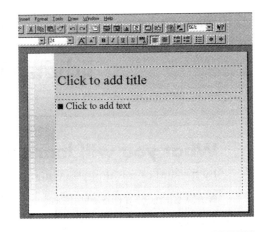

5   Click in the title box to give your slide a title. Type: Starting PowerPoint.

6   Click in the main body part of the slide to type in text.

7   Click the **New slide** button to move to the next slide, then repeat the above operations.

Adding pictures to a slide

Task 2: Adding a picture

1   Click the **New slide** button to create a new slide.

2   Choose the Text & Clipart slide layout, as in this screen.

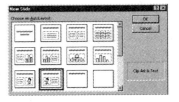

3   Click **OK**. This screen should be displayed.

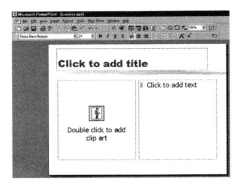

4 Double-click where indicated to include clip art. It may take a minute or two to display the clip art.

5 A screen similar to this one should appear.

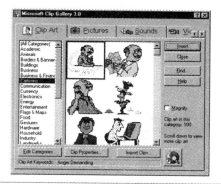

6 Scroll through the clip art images and click on the one you want to insert in your slide, then click the **Insert** button. The clip art will appear in your slide.

Note that you can select a category of clip art from the categories on the left. The clip art can be sized after it has been inserted in your slide.

You may also see a message that additional clips are available on the CD-Rom.

Adjusting the size of images

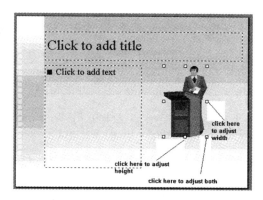

To adjust the height of the image, click where shown, hold the mouse button down and drag the mouse up or down to increase or decrease the height. Width is similarly adjusted, using the width marker as shown above.

You can adjust both height and width simultaneously by clicking the corner, as indicated, and dragging to resize.

Adjusting the position of images

To adjust the position of an image:

1   Move the mouse pointer over the image until a large white arrow pointer appears.

2   Hold down the left mouse button and drag the image to the desired position, then release the mouse button.

3   You can delete an image from a slide by clicking on the image to display its markers, then press *Delete*.

Adding other pictures to a slide

Just as you can add clip art to a slide, you can also add any other picture you have available, such as a scanned-in company logo, photograph or drawing, etc.

1   Display the slide that you want to add a picture to.

2   Drop down the Insert menu and click on Picture. A box similar to the one below will appear:

3   Choose which folder or drive to look in for your picture. By default all picture formats that can be imported will appear in the box.

4   Click on the filename of your picture, then click **OK** to insert it into your slide.

Once inserted, you can size the picture in the same way as clip art.

Adding graphs and charts to slides

To insert graphs or charts, open the application and copy the chart to the clipboard, then drop down the Edit menu and click Paste. The chart will appear in your slide, and can be positioned and sized just like any other image.

Adding shapes to a slide

PowerPoint has an AutoShapes tool on the Drawing toolbar that provides a range of shapes that can be inserted in a slide.

1   Click on the **AutoShapes** tool on the Drawing toolbar, then select the category required.

2   Double-click on the desired shape to insert it in your slide, dragging it to the position and size required.

Multimedia presentations: adding sound and video to slides

If your presentation is being run on a multimedia capable PC, you can insert short sound and video clips into slides using the **Insert** menu and suitable sound or video clips.

 You should be aware that sound and video use enormous amounts of memory and hard disk space, and presentations that use them should always be tried out on the machine that is going to be used to run the presentation. You should also beware that multimedia presentations are likely to be too large to fit onto floppy disks.

Formatting your slides

PowerPoint, like most Windows packages, allows you a great deal of control over the formatting of text, paragraphs, etc. However, since it is a presentation package, the default templates have been carefully designed to make your presentation look good. Unless you are an experienced graphic designer, it's not recommended that you change the formatting from the defaults provided.

The Format menu allows you to change characteristics such as fonts, colour schemes etc. For more information, see the PowerPoint Help Answer Wizard on Formatting.

Running presentations

What you will learn in this unit

By the end of this unit you will be able to:

- run presentations manually

- run presentations automatically

- run presentations continuously

- control transitions between slides and add special effects

- distribute presentations for use on other computers.

Running presentations manually

Task 1: Running a presentation manually

1   Start PowerPoint and open your presentation. Click View, Slide Show to display the first slide.

Don't confuse Slide view, used for editing slides, with Slide Show, for running your presentation. In Slide Show view, only your slide is visible, not the PowerPoint menus and toolbars.

2   To show all slides in sequence, use *PgDn* to advance to the next slide. *PgUp* takes you back to the previous slide.

3   To go straight to the last slide, press *End*. To go to the first slide, press *Home*.

4   To go to a particular slide, just type the slide number and press *Return*. Alternatively, if you're not sure of its number, go to Slide Sorter view, highlight the slide you want to go to and double-click.

5   To end your slide show at any time, just press *Esc*. This will take you back to Slide view.

6 To show only some of the slides, drop down the Slide Show menu and click on Hide Slide.

You can also drop down the Slide Show menu and click Set up Show to display the following screen:

Enter the starting and finishing slide numbers, then click Show.

If the slides you want to show are not in a continuous range, you can use the slide sorter to rearrange them so that the ones you want are continuous.

Running presentations automatically

Task 2: Running a presentation automatically

1 Drop down the Slide Show menu.

2 Select Rehearse Timings. Your first slide will appear, with this Rehearsal box in the bottom left corner of the screen.

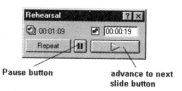

Pause button   advance to next slide button

3 When the slide has been displayed for the required amount of time, click on the **arrowhead** button to advance to the next slide.

4 To pause the clock while you think about just how long you want the slide to display, click on the **VCR Pause** button in the box.

5 When you reach the end of the slides, this box is displayed. Click the **Yes** button to save the timings.

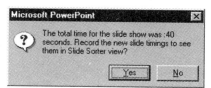

6 When you run your presentation, choose Use Timings from the Set up Show box and click **OK** .

You can still go straight to a particular slide by typing the slide number and pressing *Return*, or end the presentation by pressing *Esc*.

Running your presentation continuously

Sometimes, you may want a continuously running presentation, for example to advertise services or courses, or to display information.

■ Create timings for an automatic presentation as shown in Task 2.

■ Display the Set up Show box and click Loop Continuously, then click **Show** . Your presentation will run until you press *Esc*.

Controlling transitions between slides and adding special effects

Task 3: Controlling slide transition and adding special effects

1 Change to Slide Sorter view.

2 To apply the same effects to all slides, drop down the Edit menu and click Select All. To apply an effect to only one slide, click on the slide.

3 Click the **Transitions** button on the PowerPoint toolbar to display the Slide Transition box.

4 In the Effects box, click on the **down arrow** to display the types of slide transition available.

5 Click Slow, Medium or Fast to determine the speed of transition.

6 Choose automatic or manual transition in the Advance box. It will default to automatic for presentations that are set to run automatically.

7   Associate a range of sound effects or add your own in the Sound box.

8   Finally, click **OK** to accept your choices. A thumbnail view of the transition is shown on the black and white dog image.

9   Practise using different transition effects and sounds.

Creating a presentation to run on another computer

PowerPoint's Pack & Go Wizard allows you to distribute your presentation on disk so that it can be run on another computer, without the need for the other computer to have a copy of PowerPoint (although it will need Windows). You may find it helpful to drop down the Help menu, click Answer Wizard and type in Pack and Go for an overview.

To copy the presentation to a floppy disk, drop down the File menu and click Pack & Go. Follow the on-screen instructions.

PowerPoint will automatically compress your presentation and prompt you to insert floppy disks to store it.

More advanced features of PowerPoint

PowerPoint has many features to enhance your presentations:

■ **Organisation charts** can easily be drawn using the Organisation Chart tool.

■ **Builds** allow you to reveal the points on a slide one by one.

■ **Hidden slides** allow you to include slides dealing with those tricky questions that you hope no-one will ask!

■ **Branching** presentations allow you to select a different route through the presentation.

■ **Kiosk** applications are continuously running presentations, perhaps providing information or publicity material.

■ **Web publishing** allows you to publish presentations on the World Wide Web.

On your own

Use the Help Wizard to look up each of the above topics in bold.

Section 5
Outlook

Introduction to Outlook

What you will learn in this unit

By the end of this unit you will be able to:

■ use Outlook to make appointments

■ use Outlook to send and receive e-mail

■ use Outlook to create an electronic address book of contacts

■ use Outlook to print out your appointments, contacts, etc.

Introduction to Outlook

Outlook is an electronic diary and organiser, allowing you to create, view and organise your information.

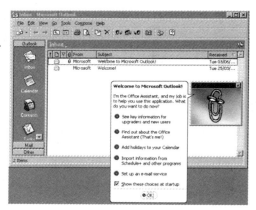

Information is stored in folders, which can be reached quickly by clicking on the appropriate shortcut in the Outlook bar.
See the screen on the right:

Inbox allows you to send and receive e-mail

Calendar is for making appointments, arranging meetings etc.

Contacts is a name and address database

Tasks is for making and reviewing To-do lists

Journal is an electronic diary, showing you all your appointments, tasks etc.

Notes is for making post-it type notes.

Outlook is intuitive to use; you simply choose the appropriate view and enter details of the appointment, etc. However, it can also be used by groups of co-workers to arrange meetings, etc. by inspecting available times on each individual worker's schedule. You can also Outlook's recurring events easily, for example to arrange team meetings at 10am every Monday. Data can also be imported to and exported from other Office applications; for example you can use Outlook for mail merging with Word.

Finally, data in Outlook can be printed out by choosing the appropriate view.

Starting Outlook

If the Office toolbar is visible, you can click on the **Outlook** button as shown below:

If the toolbar isn't visible, click on the **Start** button at the lower left of the screen taskbar, then choose Programs, Outlook. The following box will appear:

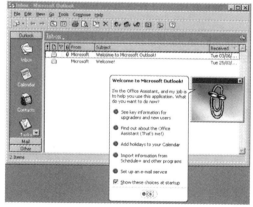

Creating a new contact

From the Office shortcut bar, click the **New Contact** button, shown in the screen below:

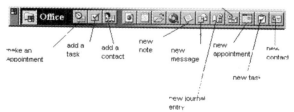

147

If the Office shortcut bar is not displayed, start Outlook from the Start, Programs menu, drop down the Outlook File menu and click New, Contact, as shown in the screen below:

When the Contact screen appears, fill in the information in the boxes then click the **Save and Close** button:

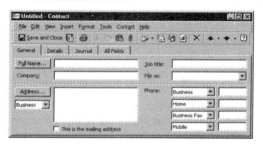

Opening and editing an existing contact

Task 1: Opening an existing contact

1   Open Outlook if it's not already open.

2   Click **Contacts** on the Outlook bar. Not the Office shortcut bar.

3   To edit information, move the cursor to the information you want to change. | If you can't edit, click the View menu, click Format View then click Allow in-cell editing.

4   Click the **Close** button at the top right of your screen.

5   Now practice using contact to add and edit some business or personal contacts of your own.

Creating and sending e-mail

Note that you must be connected to the Internet or an intranet to be able to send and receive e-mail.

Task 2: Using e-mail

1 Click the **New message** button on the Office shortcut bar or the **New message** button on the Outlook bar. This screen will appear.

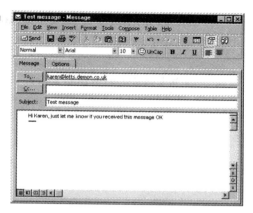

2 In the To box, fill in the e-mail address of the recipient. E-mail addresses are usually lower case.

3 In the subject box, give a brief description of what the message is about.

4 In the main window, type your message.

5 Click the **Send** button to send your e-mail (you have to be connected to the Internet to send the message). You can also send e-mails to more than one person at a time, and select addresses from address books rather than typing them in each time.

Sending a file with an e-mail: attaching a file

You can also attach a file to an e-mail message.

Task 3: Attaching a file to an e-mail

1 Repeat steps 1–4 above to create an e-mail message.

2 Click on the paper-clip **Insert file** button on the Outlook toolbar.

3 Select the drive and folder and double-click on the file to attach it.

4 Send the e-mail in the normal way.

Reading an e-mail message

Task 4: Reading a new message

1 Start Outlook.

2 Click **Inbox** on the Outlook bar. This screen will appear.

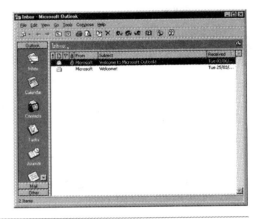

3 Double-click on the message you want to read.

4 If it is displayed, read the Welcome to Microsoft Outlook message for an overview of Outlook's features.

The Outlook Calendar

Task 5: Opening the Outlook Calendar

1 Start Outlook and click the **Calendar** button on the Outlook bar. A screen similar to this will appear.

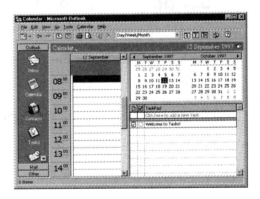

The Calendar replaces the schedule in Microsoft Schedule +, which came with Office 95. By default, Day View is displayed.

2 Click on a date to see the schedule for that day.

3 If you click to the left of one of the Sunday dates, that week's schedule will be displayed. Try it now, you should see a screen similar to this one.

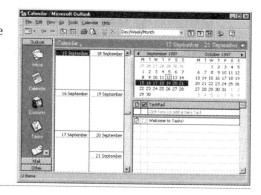

Making appointments

Task 6: Making an appointment

1 Start Outlook and open the Calendar in Daily View.

2 Select the period 10.30–12.30 with the mouse then right click to display the menu, as in this screen.

3 Click New Appointment, then fill in the other boxes as required.

4 Click the **Save and Close** button.

Recurring appointments

Task 7: Making a recurring appointment

1 To make a recurring appointment, click on the **Make Recurring** button before clicking **OK**. This box is displayed.

2 Enter the appropriate details then click **OK**.

Deleting and moving appointments

Task 8: Changing an appointment

1 Click on the appointment (it doesn't matter which view you are in) using the mouse button, then select Delete from the menu.

You can undo a deletion by dropping down the Edit menu and choosing Undo.

2 You can move appointments by right clicking on them to display the Move box, then type in the new details.

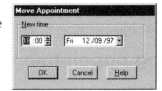

On your own

Practise using Outlook to make appointments, create contacts etc. Explore the different views.

Printing from Outlook

Task 9: Printing from Outlook

1 Drop down the File menu and click Print to display this box.

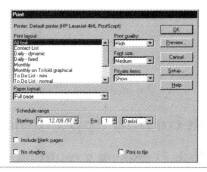

2 The box is fairly self-explanatory, so make the desired selections then click **OK**.

3 To exit from Outlook, drop down the File menu and click Exit.

Outlook is potentially a powerful groupware application, allowing you to organise and share information with your colleagues. This book has only introduced the most basic features of Outlook, leaving you to explore it more fully yourself. It is particularly useful if you already have an Internet connection or an orgnisational intranet. If you use Word as your e-mail editor, you can include many other features in your e-mails, including automatic hyperlinks and document maps. See the 'Welcome to Microsoft Outlook' message in your inbox (see the 'Reading an e-mail message' section above).

Summary of shortcuts

What follows is not meant to be a comprehensive list of commands, just a selection of tasks that are frequently performed.

Move cursor to beginning of file, worksheet, presentation or table	*Ctrl-Home*
Underline selected text	[U]
Move cursor to end of file, worksheet, presentation or table	*Ctrl-end*
Italicise selected text	[I]
Move to a new page in Word (insert page break)	*Ctrl-Enter*
Embolden selected text	[B]
Move right one screen in Excel	*Alt-PgDn*
Left-align selected text	[≡]
Move left one screen in Excel	*ALT-PgUp*
Centre selected text	[≡]
Move to a particular cell in Excel or page in Word	Edit menu, GoTo
Right-align selected text	[≡]
Cut selected text or graphics to the clipboard	[✂]
Justify selected text	[≡]
Copy selection to the clipboard	[📋]
Indent selected text	[≣]
Paste selection from the clipboard in Word, Access or Excel	[📋]

Open a file	⬚
Display/Print formulae in Excel	Tools menu, Options, View, Formulae
Save a file	⬚
Sideways printing in Excel	Preview, SetUp, Landscape
Sorting in Access & Excel	⬚
Manual re-calculation	Tools menu, Options, Calculation
Undo last action	Toolbar button or Edit menu, Undo
Switch between open applications	Taskbar or *Alt-Tab*
Spell check	⬚

Glossary

Absolute addressing
In Excel a way of storing data so that the formula is not adjusted.

Active cell
In Excel the cell with a double border around it which is the cell being worked on.

Bar chart
In Excel, a horizontal bar chart.

Clipboard
A temporary storage area.

Column chart
In Excel, a vertical bar chart.

Copying text
Making a copy of text to another place in the document while leaving the original text where it is.

Cutting and pasting
A method of moving text. Cutting text deletes it from the document and stores it in the clipboard. Pasting the text places the text from the clipboard back into the required place in the document.

Database
The electronic equivalent of a filing cabinet or card index box.

Dialog box
A window that often appears in the middle of your screen when you use menus.

Field
In a database, the equivalent to each data item in a record.

Font
A particular combination of typeface and size, e.g. Arial normal 10-point.

Functions
In Excel, shortcuts to save having to enter long or complicated formulae, for example the SUM command.

Hanging indent
Used in a list where the first line of the paragraph 'hangs out' to the left of the main body text on second and subsequent lines.

Moving text
Deleting text from its orginal location and placing it somewhere else.

Point
Measurement of font size. There are 72 points to one inch (2.5 cms).

Presentation
In PowerPoint, a set of two or more related slides.

Primary key
In Access a way of sorting records to allow fast access.

Range of data
A rectangular block of cells in a spreadsheet that is referred to by the top left cell and bottom right cell in the range.

Record
In a database, the equivalent of an indivudal card in a card index.

Report
In Access, the method used for printing out data.

Selection squares
The small black markers at each corner and mid-way along each side of a chart or other graphic which indicate that it is selected.

Sheet tabs
The tabs at the bottom of the Excel screen used to move from sheet to sheet.

Slide
In PowerPoint, one OHP slide or one screen of a presentation.

Spreadsheet
A software package used for dealing with data that is largely numerical rather than textual.

Table
In a database, the equivalent of a drawer in a filing cabinet.

Typeface
The name given to a set of letters of the alphabet, etc. in a particular style such as Arial or times New Roman.

Wizards
Step-by-step guides to producing standard documents.

Workbook
A group of one or more related worksheets.

Worksheet
An individual spreadsheet which forms part of a workbook.

Index